What others are saying about the book

"This wonderful parable really speaks to your heart, I couldn't put it down. Todd has done a masterful job of condensing servant leadership into simple and applicable truths for people of all ages." —*Wally Armstrong, Lifetime PGA tour member; bestselling author,* **The Mulligan** *(with Ken Blanchard)*

"I could not put this book down. It transcends culture, gender, economics . . . something that anyone can relate to. What a message! Simplicity in Christ is the key." —*Monty Williams, Head coach, New Orleans Hornets; author,* **Look Again 52**

"A real life changer! An incredible story packed full of great leadership insights. It grabbed my attention from the beginning. Coaches, parents, and business leaders alike will benefit tremendously from reading this book." —*Mark Merrill, President, Family First (All Pro Dad); host,* **Family Minute** *radio show*

"Engaging and compelling narrative. As a business leader I found its takeaways right on target—touching life where the rubber meets the road. I wasn't able to put it down. It's that good!" —*John D. Beckett, Chairman, The Beckett Companies; author,* **Loving Monday**

"For those seeking to win the hearts of athletes, or win in the game of life, *LEAD . . . for God's Sake!* is a real game changer. Coaches, business leaders, and parents alike will be profoundly impacted by this incredibly powerful story." —*Tony Dibenedetto, Chairman, United States Coaches Association*

"I wish *LEAD . . . for God's Sake!* had been available to my classes and seminars for business students and practitioners over the last twenty-five years. It is that good! . . . An engaging story you won't want to put down." —*Dr. John Mulford, Former dean of the school of business, Regent University*

"*LEAD . . . for God's Sake!* is the best book I have ever read . . . an incredible reminder of the gift that we have been given to lead and develop in a positive way." —*Bubba Cunningham, Director of athletics, University of Tulsa*

"*LEAD . . . for God's Sake!* is a gift that extends a gentle invitation to explore one's life and true purpose for existence. A true game changer!" —**David Rivers, Former NBA and European League basketball player; director, Village Camps Worldwide**

"Very inspirational for my own faith walk. A great message for all who read it!" —**Michael Trainor, CEO, Stratus LIVE; former CEO, Jackson Hewitt**

"I loved the book. [*LEAD . . . for God's Sake!*] was a big time inspiration to me as a coach. It truly impacted my staff and our families." —**Todd Graham, Head football coach, University of Pittsburgh**

"Incredible book! By far the best leadership book I've read in a long, long time. I read it cover to cover within days. *LEAD . . . for God's Sake!* is so needed for transforming leaders today." —**Patrick McBane, President, Marketplace Solutions**

"I have finished the book and am a raving fan. Well done! [*LEAD . . . for God's Sake!*] is a resource that will change communities, families, and lives for the better. Great job!" —**Glenn Repple, President, GA Repple and Company**

"A captivating and profound story that will reach deep into your heart." —**JD Collins, Former NCAA Final Four referee; commissioner, Mid-Central Athletic Conference**

"[*LEAD . . . for God's Sake!*] is amazing . . . I think it touches everyone in some capacity. It is a must read for anyone who deals with people and is charged with leading others." —**Tony Alford, Wide receivers coach, University of Notre Dame**

"Right on target with issues that apply to any life situation where more than one person is involved. A powerful and important message that definitely strikes a chord." —**Mike Bobinski, Associate vice president, athletics director, Xavier University**

To see more, visit www.leadforgodsake.com.

LEAD...
for
God's Sake!

by Todd G. Gongwer

Tyndale House Publishers, Inc.
Carol Stream, Illinois

Visit Tyndale online at www.tyndale.com.

Visit the author's website at www.leadforgodsake.com.

TYNDALE and Tyndale's quill logo are registered trademarks of Tyndale House Publishers, Inc.

LEAD . . . for God's Sake!: A Parable for Finding the Heart of Leadership

First printing by Tyndale House Publishers, Inc., in 2011.

Previously published by Kardia House Publishing under ISBN 978-0-9825941-0-0, Library of Congress Control Number: 2010922610.

Cover design and interior illustrations by Jeff Stillson, Stillson Studios

Edited by Jonathan Schindler

ISBN 978-1-4143-7055-2

Printed in the United States of America

17 16 15 14 13 12 11
 7   6   5   4   3   2   1

This book was written for
Kaden and Kira, and my friends in leadership

This book is dedicated to
my grandfather, Nelson Gongwer, whose love for people, fun,
and writing greatly impacted me

Table of Contents

Foreword by Urban Meyer ix

Chapter 1 *The Need to Lead* 1
Chapter 2 *The Good Life* 7
Chapter 3 *Missing Something* 19
Chapter 4 *Priorities* 31
Chapter 5 *Get Outta Here* 39
Chapter 6 *Sharing Rock Bottom* 45
Chapter 7 *Mondays with Joe* 55
Chapter 8 *The Ride Continues* 63
Chapter 9 *From the Inside Out* 71
Chapter 10 *The Real Reason* 89
Chapter 11 *Listening to Hear* 97
Chapter 12 *First Things First* 105
Chapter 13 *Searching for the Heart* 119
Chapter 14 *Never Too Late* 125
Chapter 15 *Reconciliation—A Real Gut Check* 137
Chapter 16 *Influence and Responsibility* 141
Chapter 17 *Burying the Hatchet* 155
Chapter 18 *A Real Treasure* 165
Chapter 19 *Digging Deeper* 171
Chapter 20 *Homecoming* 179
Chapter 21 *Walking Through It* 185
Chapter 22 *Celebration* 191
Chapter 23 *The Purpose Effect* 209
Chapter 24 *The Final Test* 219
Chapter 25 *What Really Matters* 227

Afterword *Joe's Book* 235
          Acknowledgments 243

Foreword

In the summer of 2011 a good friend of mine, knowing that I was in the midst of a season of reflection, gave me a copy of *LEAD . . . for God's Sake!* After explaining to me the incredible impact the book had had on his life, he assured me I would not only enjoy it, but also be impacted by its message. He was right—in a big way.

From the very start of this captivating parable, I found myself relating to the characters within. By going straight to the essence of leadership and purpose, the story challenged me to reflect upon how powerfully these two areas of life had affected not only my own pursuits and successes, but also the successes of the teams I had led in the past. Leadership and purpose were things I had dealt with a lot as we experienced success along the way. So of course, as the main characters wrestled through some of life's most important questions relating to these two subjects, I found myself doing the same, eventually following their lead to that ever-important question lying at the heart of leadership: *why do we do what we do?*

As I thought back to the whys in my own life, I was reminded of the importance of relationships and how the opportunity to positively impact lives had served as a driving force behind my decision to coach. However, as *LEAD . . . for God's Sake!* continued to unfold and painted a vivid picture of how the pressures to succeed in our culture can attack us from all angles, I was also reminded of how powerfully these pressures can affect our motives and, in turn, our leadership. Eventually, these pressures entice us to pursue success, many times at the expense of the most important things in life—relationships. In the end, the story took me, as it will take you, on an incredible adventure toward not only a better understanding of leadership and relationships, but also a better understanding of how relationships lie at the center of our purpose both in leadership and in life.

Regardless of where you are in your own personal journey, I am convinced you will be both encouraged and challenged by this book. Its message is clear, concise, entertaining, and understandable for anyone who is receptive to changing their behavior and their relationships with others.

LEAD . . . for God's Sake! was one of the most powerful books I have ever read. It gave me an instant jolt of energy and reignited a passion within me to live and lead from my true purpose in life—with relationships at the foundation of all of my pursuits. My hope is that as you read this book, you will open up not only your mind but also your heart to the life-changing ideas and principles within.

Urban Meyer
Husband, father, and former two-time NCAA National Championship–winning college football head coach

Chapter 1

The Need to Lead

"*L*EAD, for God's sake!" Coach Rocker yelled, bringing his twenty-minute tirade to an end as he stormed out of the locker room and slammed the door behind him. He was at his wits' end. This was the Knights' third loss in a row. And to make matters worse, it had come at the hands of cross-town rival Bishop South, a team they'd owned since the day Coach took over the program just three short seasons ago.

After losing in the final seconds of last year's state championship game, expectations for the Knights were sky-high coming into the 2007 season, and with good reason. Four of the five starters from that team were back, and as seniors, this was their year. It seemed the stage was set for the perfect season. Instead, the Knights were now sitting on a record of three wins and three losses, and Coach Rocker could feel the pressure of unmet expectations beginning to mount.

As one of the most successful coaches in Kentucky high school basketball history, Coach Steve Rocker was already a legend in the state. The former sharpshooting point guard from Indiana University had taken both of his previous teams to Kentucky state championships, and prior to coming to Franklin North had compiled an overall record of 356–41 in just seventeen seasons as a head coach. Emerging from the shadow of his father, the legendary Indiana high school basketball coach Pete Rocker, Steve, at just forty-two, was well on his way to becoming one of the all-time greats in his profession.

After experiencing three sub-five-hundred seasons in a row, Kentucky powerhouse Franklin North High School had hired Coach Rocker in the summer of 2005, convinced he could bring the Knights back to the glory days. Never one to disappoint, the fiery head coach had done just that by achieving a record of 14–6 in his first season with the Knights, followed by a record of 19–4, a regional championship, and a state runner-up title in his second season. Clearly, the Knights were back. Coach Rocker was practically given the key to the city, as the people of Franklin adored their beloved Knights and anyone who contributed so positively to their success. Now, in just his third season at the helm, the state championship was clearly within reach, and the standard was set. Anything less than the title for the number-one-ranked Knights would be viewed as failure in the eyes of the Franklin community—and in the eyes of Coach Rocker, too.

Coach didn't bother stopping by his office to lock up or to discuss the game with any of his assistant coaches. Although he'd typically confer with them after a game to determine the team's shortcomings, as far as he was concerned, this was all about team leadership . . . or a lack thereof. There was absolutely no other excuse. The Knights had worked their tails off all summer long. They were running their offense to perfection and, with 6' 9" All-state center David Kelton filling the lane, their defense had wreaked havoc on each of their opponents . . . in the first three games of the season, that is.

Now, for some reason, they weren't getting it done anymore. The Knights looked sloppy on both ends of the floor and out of sync in virtually every aspect of the game. Something just wasn't right, and Coach Rocker was determined to get to the bottom of it immediately.

Long after most of the fans had left the building, Coach, still stinging from the loss and submerged in his own thoughts, walked down the lonely back corridor adjacent to the gymnasium on the way to his car. As he neared the large, steel door to the outside, a lone voice rang out from behind.

"Hang in there, Coach. There's a reason for everything."

Startled, he turned to see who it was. All he could make out was a short, dark figure standing at the end of the hall, holding what looked like a mop in his hand. Although he wasn't certain, the short frame and the mop made it pretty easy to guess who it was, despite the darkness of the hallway. It had to be Joe Taylor, the school janitor.

Though Joe appeared to be a popular figure among the students, he was usually pretty reserved around Coach, so a relationship between the two men had never developed. Nonetheless, every once in a while, seemingly out of the blue, Joe would say something almost philosophical in nature. It would be brief, and maybe even a little bit confusing; but for some reason, it always seemed deeply meaningful.

"Yeah, right, Joe . . . whatever," Coach answered as he gave a halfhearted wave and turned to finish the walk to his car. "A reason for everything . . . what the heck is that supposed to mean?" he mumbled to himself.

As he made the thirty-minute drive home through the hills of eastern Kentucky, Coach continued to seethe. Questions flooded his mind. What was wrong with his team? Why did his guys not understand how important these games were? Why did they seem so clueless about leadership? Why did they just not care about winning as much as he did? Was it laziness, complacency, overconfidence?

Whatever it was, there was no excuse for it, and he was determined to make them pay. No team of his was going to lose like this ever again. Besides, they needed to understand these lessons to be successful later in life. *If you don't pursue your goals with passion, how can you expect to ever make it to the top, regardless of what you're striving for?* Deep in thought, he continued the drive through the lonely darkness of the Kentucky countryside.

Eventually, his mind shifted to considering options for the next day's practice. *Maybe we shouldn't even pick up a ball? We'll just get between the lines and run, and do defensive drills. Yep, back to basics. If these guys don't hate losing enough to work harder than they have been during games, I'll teach 'em to hate what happens in practice when they don't!* He'd seen it work before, so he was confident it would work again. He would ratchet the intensity up big time as a wake-up call they all desperately needed to hear.

As Coach pulled up to his house, he noticed Brandon, his ten-year-old son shooting baskets on the dimly lit court off to the side of the driveway. Shorter than most of his friends, Brandon was a true chip off the old block, both in stature and attitude. What he lacked in size he made up for with his determination, relentlessly pursuing his dream of following in his dad's footsteps to become a basketball superstar.

"Hey, Dad! Sorry about the loss . . . Wanna play me in one-on-one?" Brandon asked, hoping to cheer him up a bit.

"Sorry, Brandon, Dad's got to get some things done tonight before tomorrow's practice. You keep working on your game so your team never does what ours did tonight. Bunch of lazy punks . . ." he muttered, closing the door to the house behind him.

Brandon was used to this answer, so he shrugged it off pretty easily. He knew how important winning was to his dad, so anytime the Knights lost, Brandon normally stayed clear. Not sure why he'd even asked, Brandon went back to his routine of counting down the seconds to the end of the state championship game, dribbling through defenders, and hitting the shot at the buzzer. In jubilation, Brandon would jump around, imagining the fans swarming him while his dad proudly embraced him. State champs at last. That was his dream.

But now, back to reality. Even though his dad's not spending time with him was tough to take, he knew Coach had to work hard to produce winning teams, so he'd learned not to make a big deal about it. Besides, when Dad's team won, he was always in a good mood. And since he won most of the time, all was usually well—so well, in fact, that Coach Rocker was frequently being interviewed on the nightly news or written about in articles. People seemed to know him everywhere they went. It was cool having everyone worship his dad because of his basketball success. It was also cool to live in a great neighborhood in a big house. So, despite his disappointments, Brandon had learned that the lack of time with his dad was the price he had to pay for all the other great things that came with his success.

Once inside the house, Coach headed straight for his favorite stewing spot, the den, to begin the breakdown of the previous game's film. Almost immediately upon settling into his chair with his notebook in hand, the phone rang. It was Grant Steffin, Coach Rocker's favorite golfing buddy. Grant lived in a beautiful home just down the street and was the CEO of Cybelcom, one of the fastest-growing companies in the region. Before that, the Ivy League-educated business whiz had founded his own software company, which was eventually bought out by Cybelcom in the late nineties. After just three years as a division president for Cybelcom, the board recognized Grant's uncanny ability to lead and handed him the reins of the entire organization. Grant exuded confidence, and with his athletic build and thick, dark hair, he even looked the part of a leader. He truly seemed to have it all. If anyone knew about leadership or how to win, it was Grant Steffin.

"Hey, Coach. Thought you might be up for a beer," Grant said in his normal upbeat tone. "I know the loss is eatin' away at ya, so I thought I'd offer my counsel . . . along with a cold beverage, of course."

Coach could rarely turn down the opportunity to hang out with Grant, especially feeling like he was. So, despite the late hour, he accepted the invitation, jumped up from his chair, and headed for the door.

"Runnin' over to Grant's for a few!" he yelled, slipping into his jacket.

Kathy, Coach's wife, was upstairs putting Kylee, their six-year-old daughter, to bed. She popped her head out from the bedroom doorway and shot him a disgusted look. Coach knew what she was thinking, but at this point, he didn't really care. He had more important things to worry about than a nagging wife. Shrugging it off, he walked out the door and headed across the backyard, following his normal shortcut to Grant's place.

Chapter 2

The Good Life

Greeting him at the front door with his typical handshake and encouraging pat on the shoulder, Grant invited Coach in. As the two men walked through Grant's house, Coach glanced, with a bit of envy, at the mammoth entertainment center in the great room. One hundred and two inches of pure HD bliss, complete with the sound-system equivalent of an IMAX movie theater. *Must be nice*, he thought to himself. Making their way toward the basement, they passed additional telltale signs of Grant's success. From the diamond-patterned marble floors, to the rare works of art, to the pictures of Grant with all the who's who in Kentucky scattered throughout the house, it was easy to see Grant was the epitome of success.

As the men settled into the bar in Grant's basement, Grant pulled two cold brews from the fridge. After setting one in front of Coach, he twisted the cap off his own and sat down beside his friend.

"Tough one tonight, huh?" asked Grant.

"Yeah, that's an understatement," Coach replied. "The guys just don't get it. No matter how many times we go over things, or how much we reiterate our goals for this season, they still don't get it. I don't understand it. We work harder than anyone else in our district. I work harder than any coach in the state—maybe in the country. On top of that, we have arguably more talent than anyone else in the state. The only thing we don't have is leadership on the team. But I'm gonna change that tomorrow."

"Leadership . . . huh. I feel your pain, my friend," sighed Grant as he mindlessly played with the label on his beer bottle. "That's the biggest challenge with my team, too."

"Really?" asked Coach with a look of disbelief.

"Yep, *constantly* have to stay on 'em to get anything done, much less get anything done right."

Coach wondered if Grant was just yanking his chain to make him feel better. "Are you serious? With all your success, I would've thought your people would follow you over a cliff if you'd ask 'em to."

"Yeah right; I wish it were that easy. Remember, the boneheads I have to deal with every day at work are the parents of the boneheads you're dealing with every day in the gym. The only difference is, yours are worried about girls and cars, while mine are worried about families and 401ks. Come to think of it, maybe they aren't so different after all."

For the first time that evening, Coach managed to crack a smile. "So what do you do to get your leaders to lead?"

"Well, as of late, nothing seems to work. But I can tell you that in the past, I've always relied on the only thing that really works in business: the almighty dollar. That's why people come to work in the first place. Ask anyone. They'll tell you flat-out, 'gotta make ends meet.'"

Coach nodded in agreement as he took a swig of his beer.

"Of course, in today's society 'making ends meet' means a lot more than just putting food on the table for the family. Seems everybody's got to have a couple of nice cars, a nice home, all the best video games for the kids . . . It's a lot more than mere survival these days."

"So, I guess that's a good thing, right?" asked Coach. "I mean, as long as people are caught up trying to get all those nice things, they should stay really motivated for you."

"You'd think so, but it doesn't always work that way. Because eventually, they always want more, regardless of how much you give 'em. It's never enough money, or insurance, or promotions, or time off—you name it, it's never enough. So that's when you have to kick their tails. And believe me, I've had to do a lot of that in the last few months trying to get people to do their jobs." Grant shook his head, frustrated at the thought of his plight.

"Of course, when that doesn't work either, you have to just cut 'em loose . . . with no regrets. You know, send a message. But that's the name of the game. If you can't run with the big dogs, you gotta stay on the porch."

"I hear that," said Coach.

Grant continued confidently, "In business, the bottom line really is the bottom line. And the only way to really succeed is to manage that obsessively. We all have to play our role. If I want to be successful, I have to make lots of money for our shareholders, 'cause in the end, it's their money that's on the line if we lose. And if *we* lose, *they* lose . . . and if *they* lose, I get axed. It's just that simple. So the only way for me to be sure that people are doing what they're supposed to be doing is to stay on top of 'em. I reward 'em well, but I also push 'em big time. They have to know, if they screw up, there'll be hell to pay."

Grant stood up and walked over to the dartboard hanging on the wall. He picked up a piece of chalk off the tray under the scoreboard hanging next to it. Somewhat flippantly, he drew a stick figure in the middle of the scoreboard. Then, over the left hand of the stick figure, he drew what looked like a bag of treasure, and over the right hand he drew a small hatchet. He turned back toward Coach, who was now sitting at the bar with a bewildered look on his face.

"Coach, leadership in its simplest form is influence. In business, sports, or whatever, you're constantly either influencing or being influenced in some way or another. So, as a person in a formal position of leadership, it's critical that I understand what most powerfully influences or moves my people to action. You know, what makes people do what they do. And as I see it, there are really only two things: fear and rewards. As a leader, you control these two things. You're always holding the treasure in one hand and the hatchet in the other." Grant

pointed to the bag of treasure and the hatchet he'd just drawn on the chalk scoreboard.

"Now, you have to choose to use whichever one of these methods works best for you to make sure the job is getting done right. People don't just do things on their own anymore. So these are really the only two ways to get 'em to do what you want 'em to do. And getting people to do what you want 'em to do is really what leadership is all about."

Grant set the chalk down and walked back toward the bar as Coach stared at the drawing, trying his best to relate the illustration to his own leadership challenges. As soon as Grant was settled back into his seat next to Coach, he started in again.

"You won't always make a lot of friends—especially when using the hatchet—but business isn't about making friends. And when you really stop and think about it, leadership isn't either. Believe me, I've made my fair share of enemies along the way, but in the end, it's always paid off. And friends—I still got 'em, they're just different. You know, politicians, CEOs, coaches . . . successful guys like you who understand the tough choices that have to be made to get to the top. If you want to be the best in this world, you have to be willing to sacrifice a lot on the way up."

"I'll drink to that," Coach said, raising his bottle in agreement.

"The bottom line is this," said Grant. "If you want leaders on your team, you have to push 'em hard, but pay 'em well, period. By the way, how much are you paying your players?" In an instant the somber tone of the conversation dissipated as both men laughed at the thought of Coach paying his high school athletes.

"Seriously, though," said Grant, "winning in sports is pretty much the equivalent to incentives in business. The harder or smarter you play, the more wins you get. The motivating factors can be just as powerful, too. Some people want to win as much, if not more, than they want to make money.

It just depends on what's most important to you, how you define success."

"You know, that's a really good point," replied Coach. "My guys don't feel the incentive of winning is big enough right now. It just doesn't mean that much to 'em anymore because they've won so much in the past. All they're worried about now is getting their points, or assists, or whatever."

Coach sighed and shook his head in frustration. "In their minds, they're already successful enough as a team, evidenced in how complacent and selfish . . . and downright lazy they played tonight. And that's why I plan on making their lives miserable tomorrow at practice." Coach's voice began to rise with emotion. "If winning isn't enough incentive for 'em, then the fear of losing—you know, the 'hatchet'—will be." Coach stood pointing at Grant, as if trying to convince him of his seriousness. "Tomorrow will be a tough practice for the whole team. But for my seniors, the guys who are *supposed* to be my leaders, it'll be hell. They need to learn that success in this world has a price. I absolutely cannot tolerate losing anymore!" Grant nodded in support of his friend and hopped up to grab a couple more drinks from the fridge.

Settling himself a bit, Coach sat back down and decided to shift the conversation to what he thought was a lighter subject. "By the way, Grant, how's the family?"

Immediately Grant's expression dropped. "Well . . . Cindy and I are really struggling right now. In fact, she moved out just last week . . . her and the kids, actually."

Caught completely off guard, Coach fumbled to find the right words in response to the bomb Grant had just dropped on him. "Uh . . . wow, Grant . . . I'm sorry. I knew you guys had your share of problems, but I had no idea . . ."

"Ah, it's okay," Grant interrupted. "It was time. I could never please her. Or the kids, for that matter. Gave 'em the world. Look at this place! Anyway, she's already talking about filing, and her bloodsuckin' lawyer is supposed to be in contact with me next week with more details."

Coach couldn't help but think about his own son, who was best friends with Grant's ten-year-old son, Michael. "So, you staying here or is Cindy?"

"I'm staying. She wants the lake house. So, as of now, it looks like they'll be moving to Lake Barkley."

"Wow. Brandon will be crushed."

"Yeah, I know. It'll be pretty hard for Michael, too. Christopher, he's a different story completely. We've lost all control of him. All he wants to do is hang out with his friends, play video games, and party. He's really messed up right now, but that's a whole other story I'd rather not get into. He takes after his mom, I guess.

"I just don't know where we went wrong with him. He used to be such a good kid. Never heard anything out of him . . . always responsible. I know the time I spent on the road was tough on him, but it's not like he didn't have plenty to do while I was gone. I don't know, maybe I was too tough on him? I just never imagined he'd end up like this . . ." Grant's voice trailed off as he spoke painfully of his son's problems.

Pausing to take another drink, Grant rolled his eyes and shifted into a more cynical tone. "Of course, Cindy blames it all on me. Yep . . . I guess everything's *my* fault."

"Any chance you guys might try and work it out?" asked Coach.

"Nah . . . it's not worth it. She's fed up with the long hours and the time I spend at the office. Says it's like the kids haven't had a dad for the last five years anyway. Not to mention the fact she thinks I'm an alcoholic, which I'm not. But I guess her perception is her reality so . . . whatever."

Coach immediately looked down at the bar to avoid eye contact. He'd always wondered if Grant had a drinking problem but didn't want to get into it now.

"I just don't get people like her. I bust my ass my whole life to give her everything she's ever dreamed of, and then, when she finally gets it . . . bam! She's out the door."

Coach shook his head in empathy. "Well, if it's any consolation, Grant, Kathy isn't especially thrilled with my schedule either. She's constantly on me about spending more time with the kids. But you know what? That's just the way it is. I didn't become the winningest coach in Kentucky basketball history by sitting around the campfire with my family and friends every night singing kumbaya. Besides, my dad never spent a lick of time with me when I was growing up, and I turned out all right. It made me tough. Taught me to fight for what I really wanted. My mom never hounded him much either. 'Course, they split up when I was twelve. But the fact still remains: if you want to make it in our society—I mean be a real 'impact player,' as I like to call 'em—you have to pay the price."

Nodding his head in agreement, Grant couldn't resist adding his two cents. "Yep, our wives just don't get it, and I don't think they ever will."

"Unfortunately, my *team* doesn't get it either," said Coach. "They want all the great things success in this world has to offer, but they're not willing to pay the price. I just don't understand that way of thinking. Of course, their parents only make matters worse. They coddle the kids their whole lives, waiting on them hand and foot; then, as soon as something gets a little challenging in life, they jump to the rescue. God forbid the kid learn anything the hard way! Sacrifice for the good of their teammates? Are you kidding me? *'Not my little Johnny . . . this life is all about him!'*"

Coach was oozing with cynicism now, too. "Why does it seem like I'm the only one who cares about whether these kids learn how to be leaders or be successful in this life? That's the real reason we have no leadership on our team: the parents don't teach 'em a d— thing at home 'cause they're too busy doing their own thing. All the while, the kids sit around the house watching *Cribs* on MTV thinking they'll have a huge 'crib' like that someday, too. All they think they have to do is look pretty. They fail to connect the dots, the dots that just happen to get you from point A to point B in life. If you want a house like that, or like the one we're sitting in right now—" he smiled and winked at Grant—"you gotta be willing to sacrifice . . . a lot."

"No doubt," said Grant. "Believe me: hundreds of folks who work for me have the same mentality. They want to come in, punch the clock, and get out, as quick and easy as possible. They do just the minimum to get by each day and then they're out the door. All they care about is their paycheck. Would you believe last month we did an audit and caught fifty-four people throughout the company cheating on their time cards? Fifty-four! No regard for the company. It's like they hate being there. And we pay them better than any of our competitors. Still, all they want is to get that paycheck on Friday and get out the door."

Grant stood up again, agitated at the thought of how his people had been acting. "And then they want a raise because they showed up for work six months straight without missing a day. What kind of achievement is that? I thought that's what the employment agreement was in the first place: you do *this* and the company agrees to pay you *that*. But it's never enough! And it's this way throughout the company. Even the employees making six figures have this mentality. They're happy at bonus time, but three months later, if they get a shot at a little more money somewhere else, they'll jump to a competitor in a heartbeat. No loyalty, no commitment anymore. It's all about me, me, me!" The redness now showing on Grant's face made it clear that this struck a deep nerve.

"People today all want the best of the best, but aren't willing to do a d— thing for it! I just don't get it." Grabbing Coach's empty beer bottle along with his own, Grant walked over to the trash and angrily threw the bottles into the receptacle before walking over to the fridge to pull out a couple more.

Still fired up, Coach chimed in again. "Yeah, we're definitely a society bent on entitlement. Something for nothing is what it's all about nowadays." He paused for a second as he twisted the cap off the cold beer Grant had just handed him. "And I don't know what will ever change this way of thinking. I guess as leaders, we need to just keep doing what we do. If others don't figure it out, it'll be survival of the fittest at its best. Only the strong will survive, baby!" Both men chuckled at the comment.

"I'm not gonna let this group of seniors ruin the record I've worked so hard to achieve over twenty years," Coach continued. "If they won't learn to lead their teammates, I'll find guys who will. Guys who are willing to step up to the plate . . . with a real hunger to win, to achieve success. Guys who *want* to lead!"

As both men took a breather from the conversation, the ticking of the blue-and-white neon Wildcat clock hanging on the wall above the bar sink caught Coach's attention. "Yikes! It's almost 1:30. Kathy's going to think I got lost running through the neighborhood. I really need to get home."

Finishing his drink, Coach took one more glance at the chalk drawing on the scoreboard. The image of the treasure and the hatchet really did make a lot of sense to him now.

"I really like that hatchet-treasure example, Grant. To my team, winning really is the treasure. It's our primary motivator. And there's no question that my guys have lost their drive to win because they've won so much in the past. Now all they want is individual 'wins' . . . which just doesn't cut it on a team. So since our 'treasure' isn't working anymore, the only other option, really, is to use the hatchet." Grant nodded as they both headed toward the stairs.

"It's just too bad it's come down to this. These kids have no idea what they have right now, a chance to really make a mark—to win a state championship. They could graduate as one of the most successful groups of guys ever to come through this program. Instead, all they want to do is bask in the glory of what they've already done."

Coach sighed as he walked through the entryway and out the front door. He turned back toward Grant. "Thanks again, Grant."

"Hey, my pleasure, Steve. I'm always up for a little late-night pep talk . . . and a few drinks, too. I just hope things go better for you tomorrow," Grant said as he shook Coach's hand and gave him his usual pat on the shoulder.

"Oh, they will," Coach answered confidently, jumping off the porch. "You can be sure of that. I'm taking my hatchet with me, so the boys'll definitely learn a thing or two about leadership and success by the end of practice tomorrow." Coach turned and began the jog back across the neighborhood to his house.

Chapter 3

Missing Something

True to his word, Coach led a fierce practice on Saturday. Complete with lots of sprints, defensive slide drills, and the occasional trip to the trash can to get rid of the day's breakfast, practice was all Coach had wanted it to be and more. There was no doubt; the message was sent loud and clear: Play like you played last night ever again, and you will pay a dear price.

In the locker room afterward Coach tried to tone it down a bit; however, upon pulling his seniors aside to give them a special lecture, his anger again got the best of him. "Guys, I get sick to my stomach when I think about how poorly you played last night! Not because you missed some easy shots, or because you made stupid mistakes. No. What really makes me sick is your selfishness. All you care about is Y-O-U. And it shows. It shows by your lack of focus, your lack of hustle, your lack of execution, and of course, it shows on the scoreboard at the end of the game."

Still dripping with sweat from the brutal practice, the four seniors stood shoulder to shoulder in the far corner of the dingy locker room as their coach continued to pelt them with words carefully aimed to pierce their hearts.

"I've worked too hard for the past twenty years to watch my record get shredded to bits because a bunch of selfish seniors don't give a rip about winning. Last I checked, winning ranked pretty high on all of your preseason goal lists. Or did I miss something? If I don't see a change soon, I'll make a change myself—and it won't be pretty. There's nothing in my contract that tells me I have to start any of my seniors. And right now, you guys are nothing to me but a bunch of spoiled prima donnas. David—especially you."

David Kelton, the Knights' senior superstar who'd already committed to play for the University of Kentucky after his senior year, was a fairly quiet kid who grew up in a middle-class neighborhood on the same side of town where Coach lived. Although he'd always been a pretty hard worker on and off the court, over the past couple of games even he seemed to be just going through the motions.

Coach turned to his star player and walked toward him, stopping just inches from his face. "As far as I'm concerned, as soon as you committed to UK, you punched your ticket and decided to coast. How can you let your teammates down like this? You're pathetic!" David winced as his Coached yelled the words two inches from his face. "Do you have any idea why we're struggling so much right now? There's absolutely no leadership on this team, and especially none from you. No one wants to step up and pay the price. If I've said it once, I've said it a hundred times, David: Step up and lead. *LEAD*, for God's sake, will ya!"

Coach backed up a couple of steps and refocused on the rest of the seniors. "And that goes for the rest of you lazy bums, too. All I can say is, you better all come ready to play next game, or things are only gonna get worse!" Turning to walk out, Coach shot an angry look toward a couple of the other players who were standing off to the side listening to the outburst. Then he stormed out through the locker room doorway and into the hall, slamming the door behind him.

Still fuming, Coach took his first step out into the hallway. Unfortunately for him, it was a step onto a freshly mopped floor. As his right foot slid forward, his left foot went backward, sending him into an uncontrollable spin, where his failed attempt to catch himself landed him flat on his butt in the middle of the hallway. As he tried to gather himself and quickly jump back up, he scanned the area, hoping no one saw his acrobatics. No such luck. To his dismay, he felt a gentle hand grab his right arm in an attempt to help him up. It was Joe, the school janitor.

"I—I'm so sorry, Coach. I just finished mopping this area and was about to put the wet floor sign up. Are you okay?" Joe was obviously shaken by the site of the hard spill Coach had just taken right in front of his eyes.

"I think I'll live," sneered Coach, both embarrassed and frustrated.

"Seriously, Coach, are you really okay?" Joe asked again, as if now inquiring after something more than just a physical injury.

Coach sighed. "Well, to tell you the truth, I just put the guys through probably the toughest practice of their lives, and then topped that off by blasting my seniors for the last ten minutes about their selfishness and lack of leadership. So actually, the fall is the least of my worries right now." Coach leaned down and began to pick up the papers that had fallen out of his folder.

Joe pressed the discussion. "Ah . . . selfishness and leadership. Two of my favorite subjects," he said, kneeling down to help Coach pick up his papers.

"Your favorite subjects?" asked Coach. "You mean you teach here, too?"

"Well, not officially," said Joe. "But I do consider that to be one of my responsibilities in life . . . teaching, that is." Joe grimaced as he struggled to get back to his feet after handing Coach the last of the papers that had fallen onto the floor. There was no doubt—Joe was a compassionate thinker. And although he'd spent the last twenty-five years of his career cleaning up after high school kids, there was something unique about him that was really starting to intrigue Coach.

Hesitating for a moment, Coach decided to probe a bit deeper. "Okay, I have to ask, why are selfishness and leadership your favorite subjects?"

Joe politely corrected Coach. "I didn't say favorite. I said two of my favorites."

"Okay. Why are they *two* of your favorites?" asked Coach in frustration.

"Well, for one, they both have a profound effect on our lives each and every day. In addition, they're really inter-connected when it comes down to it. Think about this: Your day is full of choices . . . what to eat, where to go, how to talk, all kinds of things like that. Most of those choices involve a kind of choice within the choice: Do I simply choose what I want, or do I consider what's best for others while I consider what I want? When you choose what's best for others first, you're choosing to be selfless. Choose what you want without considering others and, obviously, you're being selfish."

This was clearly something Joe had thought long and hard about, since his delivery seemed almost rehearsed.

"Now leadership," said Joe, "ah yes, that's a whole other story. One that's pretty hard to describe in just a sentence or two. But let me say this: If you're influencing, you're leading, and we're surrounded by people who influence us every day, just like we influence them. So, when you consider the choices you make each day, you should also consider the influence those choices will have on others. That's assuming you don't want to be a selfish leader," chuckled Joe, as he finished setting out the "Wet Floor" pylons.

"Coach, do you know that throughout history the number-one factor that separated the good leaders from the greatest ones was selfishness?"

Coach looked at Joe a bit cockeyed, the discussion now starting to wear on his patience.

"Yep," said Joe, wiping his hands clean with the towel he always carried around his belt. "Selfishness is the great differentiator, as I like to call it. Some leaders get it; but unfortunately, most don't, especially in our culture today. Too bad, though, 'cause in the end, the ones who do get it are the only ones who really live and lead the good life. You know, the life that really matters . . . in the long run, that is." Joe grabbed the handles of his supply cart and turned to Coach.

"Coach, I know things are tough for ya right now, but hang in there. There's a reason for everything. You just have to find it." And with that, Joe turned and headed back down the hallway.

"Uh, *right*, Joe. Thanks for the encouragement. I think." He turned the opposite direction to walk to his car.

There it was again, that *reason* thing Joe had mentioned after their last loss. *What the heck is he saying?* thought Coach. He walked through the back door of the gym and into the cool, night air.

An absolute disaster—that was the only way to describe the team's next loss against Lincoln Central. And although the Knights recovered and managed to break their four-game losing streak by winning the next two, with their 5–4 record they were still struggling far beyond their original expectations for the 2008 season.

Two and a half weeks had passed since the first "hatchet" practice, as Coach referred to it, and although there had been numerous practices similar to that first infamous practice, nothing seemed to work. Coach hadn't slept a full night in almost a month. And the speeches—well, they continued to get tougher and tougher.

During one practice, Coach took the hatchet to a new level. Brant Stevens, the Knights' lone starting junior, took an off-balance shot with defenders hanging all over him just five minutes after Coach had finished yelling at the team about shot selection. It was too much for Coach to take. In a fit of rage, he turned and kicked over the cooler sitting behind him on the bleachers. A huge splash of Gatorade instantly flooded the sidelines and made its way out to mid-court as the guys stood watching in wide-eyed amazement. Fortunately, Joe happened to be checking in on practice that day, as he often did. In an instant he was mopping up the mess Coach had made. And, as usual, he did so without any complaints. That was just how he worked.

Regardless of who caused what, Joe always displayed a positive attitude. In fact, if you stood close enough to him while he worked, you'd frequently hear him humming his favorite tunes of years past. He seemed to enjoy whatever he was doing, and it showed, not only in his attitude, but in the quality of his work. He was a great janitor, maybe the best the school had ever had. Most who knew him would say he was a borderline perfectionist by the way he took extra care to do every job to the best of his ability. Joe was a true picture of someone who worked with all of his heart.

Unable to overcome the distraction of the cooler incident, Coach brought practice to an abrupt end and decided to head home early for the evening. Driving almost thoughtlessly through the familiarities of his neighborhood, he noticed Grant taking the trash out to the curb for pickup. He stopped and lowered the window. "Hey, Grant. How's everything?"

"Just great," Grant said, with a cynical tone in his voice. "If I were any better, I'd be you."

Coach chuckled and shot back, "If you were me, you wouldn't even be able to *joke* about being great."

"That bad, huh?" asked Grant.

"Grant . . . I've lost more games in the past three weeks than I did all last year. Does that tell you anything?"

"Well, at least you have a family to go home to," said Grant in an attempt to one-up Coach's troubles.

"Rough, huh?" Coach replied, sympathy in his voice.

"Yeah . . . lotta rough stuff going on right now. You got time for a cold one?"

Coach knew he hadn't spent any time with his own family over the last month, as dealing with all the turmoil of the season was really taking its toll on them all. *But this is a friend in need*, he thought. *How can I turn him down?* "Sure, just a quick one," he answered, pulling into Grant's drive and shutting the car off.

It was unseasonably warm, so, wanting to enjoy the weather, the two men settled onto the back porch by the pool. Coach broke the silence. "Things not going so well at Cybelcom either, huh?"

"Not exactly. The economy's been killing us. So, of course, as profits tank, so too do bonuses, raises, hours . . . pretty much everything that really matters to our employees. True to form, we've lost some really good people as a result, people I thought really cared about their work . . . and our company. Unfortunately, as we talked about a few weeks ago, the only thing people really care about is their paycheck. Start messing with that, and they start runnin' for the doors." Grant's mind seemed to wander off for a second.

"You know, I really wish there were more to it. You know, that people worked for more than just that. That they came to work every day because they really *wanted* to come to work, not because they *had to* in order to survive."

"You really think that's possible," asked Coach, "I mean, for the masses? You and I may want to come to work, or at least we *used* to when things were going a little better, but do you really think that all your people could actually operate that way?"

Grant looked up from where he was sitting and gave a sigh of discouragement. "Probably not. But if I thought there was a way they could, at this point in my life, I think I'd be willing to try it. Sometimes I really feel bad for 'em," Grant said. "I guess I think it's partially my fault, my responsibility, you know, as their leader, to give 'em something more to hope for."

It was clear by the look on Grant's face that the events of the past month were starting to wear on him and cause him to question some of his original thoughts about his responsibility in leadership. "For whatever reason, lately my life just feels kind of empty. Like something's missing."

"Really?" said Coach. "Well, let me know when you find whatever it is, 'cause I'm probably missin' it, too." They both laughed.

"Seriously, don't you ever wonder if there's more to it all . . . more to what we do every day?" asked Grant.

"Actually, I've probably thought more about that in the last month than I have in the last ten years," confessed Coach as he leaned back and kicked his feet up on the lounge chair he was sitting on.

"The fact remains, Grant, I have a job to do, and that's to make sure my team is equipped to win. You have a job to do, too, and that's to make sure your company makes a profit— you know, wins. I guess whatever we can work into the mix after that primary objective is achieved is icing on the cake, right?"

Grant nodded in agreement, but with an unconvinced look on his face replied, "Yeah, I guess you're right. But it still seems like there should be more to it . . . a deeper reason. A deeper reason for doing what we do than just wins or profits."

Coach looked at him. "What did you just say?"

"I said there has to be something more to what we do . . . you know, a deeper reason."

"That's the third time . . . well, fourth time, now that you repeated it, that I've heard that phrase in the last three weeks," said Coach.

"What phrase?" asked Grant, sitting up in his chair.

"The one about a deeper reason. Our school janitor keeps saying that to me at the most inopportune times. As if I'm supposed to know what it all really means. Of course there's a reason for everything that happens. But I don't think that's what he's talking about. I think maybe he's talking more about what you just said, Grant. You know, a deeper reason *why*— why we do what we do, or even why we exist."

Coach paused for a second in deep thought and then spoke up again. "I guess I thought the treasure and the hatchet were the answers to that question, Grant. At least that's what we talked about a few weeks ago. I mean, it all really makes sense. We're either driven by the prospect of success through wealth or wins, or we're driven by a fear of losing those things, or pain or failure. That's it, right?" asked Coach, fishing for confirmation from Grant.

"Yeah, that's it . . . I guess that's the real reason we do what we do," said Grant. "At least what we talked about. But it still seems like something's missing."

"Grant, I can see what you're saying, but I don't see how you can possibly feel that way. I mean, look around you. The house, the cars, powerful friends . . . You're CEO of one of the most respected companies in the U.S. What could *you* possibly be missing?" asked Coach, trying his best to encourage Grant.

"Things aren't always what they seem, Steve; you know that. My family's a wreck, the company's profits are down, shareholders are breathing down my neck—everybody wants a piece of me. Or what I have, that is . . ."

Grant stood up and walked over to the perfectly landscaped rock waterfall cascading down into the pool and peered silently into the water with his hands in his pockets. "Sometimes I really do wonder why I do what I do . . . or for that matter, why I even exist."

Coach, feeling a bit uncomfortable now with the topic at hand, and with Grant's vulnerability, shifted in his chair and decided to try to lighten the mood a bit. "You know, Grant, they have specialists for times like this; they're called shrinks."

Grant smiled halfheartedly. "Yeah, sorry, I know I'm dumping a lot on you . . . especially given that you're going through your own hell right now too."

"Really, Grant, it's okay. Believe me: I can relate. It's just that right now, I can't worry about all the touchy-feely things in life. Right now, it's all about survival for me. If I—I mean, if we lose one more game, I might be looking for a new job at the end of the season. And I really don't want to do that, especially at this stage of my life."

Grant gave an understanding nod. "Yeah, I definitely know what you mean, 'cause for the first time in my twenty-plus years in business, I could be facing the same thing."

"Aw, you'll bounce back. Just keep doing what got you where you are today. Remember, hatchet-treasure. It'll all come back around eventually." Coach stood up and began to slowly walk back toward the gate in the fence. "I hate to say this, but I gotta run. Just remember, Grant, as Joe says, 'Hang in there; there's a reason for everything.'" His voice oozed with sarcasm. Both men chuckled and waved as the gate swung closed behind Coach, who was now jogging back to his car.

Even though Coach was smiling at the end of the conversation, deep down, he too was struggling, especially with the whole reason comment Joe and Grant had made. *Maybe there really is more to it,* he thought as he drove the car down the street and pulled into his driveway.

Chapter 4

Priorities

That night Coach stayed up late breaking down the game film of the Knights' next opponent, the Springston Tigers. If the guys wouldn't respond, he would, by studying the tape to ensure he'd know everything there possibly was to know about the Tigers.

Around midnight, Coach felt a hand on his shoulder. Startled, he turned around to find a pajama-clad little boy staring at him. Brandon was still awake.

"Hey, Dad," Brandon said sheepishly. "How come you're up so late?"

"I was just going to ask you that same thing," replied Coach.

"I don't know. I just can't sleep . . . I guess I'm just worried about things," said Brandon.

"Worried about things? Like what?" asked Coach, doing his best to shift gears into father mode.

"You know . . . just things." He paused, obviously nervous about sharing what was really bothering him. "I . . . I guess I'm worried about you and Mom. I mean, it never seems like you guys like to hang out together anymore . . . like you used to, anyway."

Coach knew immediately where this was going. Brandon was crushed when he heard Michael was moving with his mom

31

to their lake house because his parents were splitting up. What's more, he knew how hurt and scared Michael was as a result of the split. Naturally, Brandon was scared to death at the thought of this happening to his mom and dad, too. Brandon had listened closely to the last few arguments they'd had over the time Dad was spending in the gym and in his office. He'd also noticed the frustration in Mom's voice almost any time the two of them talked. It seemed liked an argument broke out every time they tried to discuss anything. Finally, they seemed to be avoiding each other at all costs, which was the hint that really tipped him off. Putting two and two together, Brandon feared the worst.

"Brandon, Mom and I still love each other. It's just that right now I'm going through a really tough time with coaching. If I don't do something about it soon, we won't even be able to think about winning our district conference, let alone state. I may not even have a job at the end of the season if things don't change soon. And if I don't have a job . . . we'll have to move until I find one. And none of us want that." Coach raised his eyebrows, looking for a sign of agreement from his son.

Brandon looked up at his dad briefly and gave a half-hearted nod.

Coach continued. "Mom sometimes doesn't really understand the pressures I'm facing. In fact, most people don't. They have no idea what it's like when everybody expects you to be winning and you're not. I have a lot to live up to, Brandon, and I don't plan on letting everyone down." Again, with shoulders slumped, Brandon gave a half nod to his dad to appease him.

"I've worked hard to win in the past, and I've worked hard to get our family where we are today . . . living in a nice house in a neighborhood like this, and having lots of nice things to go along with it. None of it came easy—you'll find that out some day. Sometimes you just have to bite the bullet . . . you know, suck it up and do whatever it takes. *That* is the only way to be a real success in this life, son. No one's going to hand it to you. You have to set your sights on what you want and then go after it as hard as you can. Does that make sense?" Coach asked, giving Brandon his first chance at an actual reply.

"Yeah, Dad. It makes sense . . . I just wish you could do all those things and still have time to play me in one-on-one once in a while. Or maybe just sit with Mom on the porch after dinner and watch me shoot baskets like you used to. I guess I just miss those things." Brandon's voice tapered off in obvious disappointment.

"I know you do, and I do, too," said Coach. "But if I win the state championship this year, it'll all be worth it. Then we'll have time to play more one-on-one. But right now, you need to get some sleep, or you'll be too tired to ever play one-on-one with me again." Still frustrated and in no mood to smile at his dad's attempt at humor, Brandon turned and headed back to bed.

Coach sat in silence, thinking about his conversation with Brandon. He felt bad that Brandon was hurting. And that he and Kathy were not getting along well either. He knew the strain on his family was growing, but he also knew he'd been here before, so he reminded himself that all he had to do was get back to winning and everything would be all right again.

His thoughts went back to his conversation with Grant and the discussion about that whole *reason* thing. What was it about that comment that kept popping back into his head? Of course there was a reason for everything. God was in control—he knew that, at least somewhere deep down. And although Coach wasn't a religious freak like some folks he knew, he'd always believed in God and that he was ultimately in control. But this *reason* thing seemed to be more than just that. Maybe it was the way Joe said it, or his timing. Or maybe, just maybe, it had something to do with that question Grant was struggling with, the one about *why* we do what we do, or for that matter, why we even exist. Whatever it was, deep in his heart, it was really starting to bother him.

On the other side of town, in a plush corner office on the tenth floor of the Cybelcom building, Grant was at his desk working away. After his conversation with Coach earlier that evening, he'd decided to go back into the office to get a jump on the next day. He, like Coach, had been burning the candle at both ends to try to pull things back together at work. So, with his family falling apart, Grant buried himself in what mattered most to him now: success at Cybelcom.

Determined to set the tone for his team, Grant sat in front of his computer, banging out e-mails to his subordinates. He'd always felt it was his responsibility to communicate the most extreme measures of commitment to his team. So when his e-mails were flying around at all hours of the night, he rested easier knowing that the message of his expectations was being sent loud and clear.

Suddenly, over the monotonous sound of his fingers tapping on the keyboard, a loud thud startled Grant, causing him to nearly fall out of his chair. "What the—?" Turning toward the open doorway to the conference room adjacent to his office, he saw nothing.

"I'm sorry. I didn't know you were in here, sir," came a voice from the back of the room. "I usually don't expect to see anyone here at this hour of the night." A short, stocky woman, looking to be in her late fifties, emerged and stood in the open doorway. She was one of the ladies from the company's cleaning service.

"I can finish this one later if you'd prefer, sir?" she asked politely.

"No worries. You're not bothering me . . . at least not now that I'm over the initial shock," replied Grant, still trying to collect himself after the chills that had shot up his spine just moments before.

"You do realize it's almost midnight, right?" said the woman in a somewhat motherly manner.

"Yeah, I know. I just have a lot pressing me right now . . . trying to stay ahead of the curve, if you know what I mean," said Grant.

"I guess," said the woman, as she hoisted a trash bag over her shoulder and walked through Grant's office toward the door. "Hope you don't get too far ahead of the curve . . . else you might just run right off the road," she mumbled under her breath as she walked into the hallway and put the bag down.

Grant, a bit shocked by the comment, couldn't resist firing back at her, "What's that supposed to mean?"

"Oh, no offense, sir. But . . . well, you know, those long hours . . . they can be pretty rough on family life . . . and on the health, and on the—well, I'm sure you know what I mean." Fearful she was bothering Grant, the cleaning woman turned to walk back into the conference room to finish her task.

"Yes, I know what you mean," said Grant, a bit defensive at the presumptuous remarks that this woman he'd never met had had the guts to make to him, the CEO of the company. "But there's a price for success in this world, you know. And if you want to really make it, so you don't have to work all your life, you have to pay the price. Besides, this whole company is following my lead. What I do and how I act trickles down throughout the organization. If I expect everyone else to dedicate their life to this place, I better be willing to do it myself first." Grant finished his sentence, feeling emboldened by the thought of everything riding on his shoulders.

The woman stopped, tilted her head, and nodded as if listening, but not necessarily agreeing. "Interesting," she said. "Guess you gotta do what you gotta do." Again, as she turned away she mumbled under her breath, "Just hope you're doing it for the right *reasons.*"

Grant looked up from his computer and thought. *The right reasons?* He sat in silence for a moment, wondering whether he should continue the conversation or get back to work.

He couldn't resist. After all, for some reason this woman had an unusual confidence about her that piqued his interest.

He got up from his chair and followed her back into the conference room. "Hey miss . . . uh, what's your name?"

"Holden. Betty Holden. But please, call me Betty."

"Okay, Betty, just so you know, I heard what you said as you walked through the door. That thing about 'doing things for the right *reasons.*' Well, now I have a couple questions for you. What's the reason you do what *you* do? I mean, you're in here after midnight night after night cleaning up all our messes. And don't get me wrong, you guys are phenomenal—in fact, best service we've ever had. But why do you do what you do, night after night?" Grant was feeling better now as he thought he had taken back control of the conversation.

"Well, it's simple . . . and yet complicated at the same time," she said as she skillfully and rather gracefully dusted the bookshelf. "There really are lots of reasons I do what I do. I *do* need a paycheck to put food on the table for my family,

so of course, that's one reason. And I've always enjoyed cleaning things up . . . and I think I'm pretty good at it, too, so
that's another reason. I get a sense of accomplishment when
cleaning, too, so that's another reason. But the real important
reasons . . . well, they would probably sound a little funny to
you, so maybe we should just stop there." She walked over to
the credenza in the corner and carefully began dusting it off
with her feathered wand.

"No, seriously, I want to know the funny reasons too."
Grant followed her over to the credenza attentively.

"Well, let's just say that at the heart of things, I work for
a great company and, truth be known, I also work for the
most incredible leader you could ever imagine. So, I guess for
simplification purposes, you could say I do what I do because
I love the people I work with and especially who I work for."

"Interesting," said Grant. "I assume you make pretty good
money then, too?"

Betty chuckled at his assumption. "Well, let me say this:
there's no doubt, the pay is incredible."

Grant smirked as he'd finally gotten to the answer he was
looking for. "Exactly! You make good money, so it's easy to like
doing what you do."

At this comment Betty immediately stopped her dusting
and turned to Grant with a stern look in her eyes. "Honey, I
said the *pay* is incredible, I didn't say anything about *money.*" No
sooner had she finished her statement than her cell phone rang.

"Excuse me, please; I have to take this. It's one of my partners on the third floor." In less than thirty seconds she clicked
off the phone. "Mr. Steffin, I hate to cut off our conversation,
but I'm needed on the third floor, and I am pretty much finished up here anyway. Do you mind?"

"Not at all. Is everything all right down there?" Grant asked.

"Oh yes, everything's fine. Certain things just take a little more teamwork, and we all have to be there for each other when those things come up. It was nice talking to you, though. I hope you get out of here before the sun comes up. Ya know—that sleep thing we're all supposed to do once a day. It really is pretty important." She winked at Grant as she gathered her cleaning supplies and slowly pushed her cleaning cart out the door.

Grant sat back down at his desk and pulled up his e-mails as he continued to mull over his conversation with the intriguing cleaning woman. He just couldn't stop thinking about her comments . . . about the pay being incredible, but not having anything to do with money, and about working for a great company—and for a great leader. These things boggled his mind, especially at this hour of the night.

Grant had always heard good things about Servileader, the giant cleaning service that Cybelcom had contracted to clean their office building. Not only were they one of the biggest cleaning service companies in the country, but they were also one of the best. Their people always did excellent work, and at a very competitive price. *There really is something different about that company,* Grant thought to himself. *They must just have a lot of great people working for 'em . . . wish we could get people like that to work for us.*

After noticing the clock on his computer screen, which read 1:00 a.m., Grant decided to shut things down for the night. He'd finally hit the wall—especially after being reminded of the all-important sleep he'd been getting so little of the past few weeks.

Chapter 5

Get Outta Here

The rain pelted the windshield of Coach's car as he wound his way through the darkness to Franklin North High School. At 5:15 in the morning the gloomy weather only added to the sourness of the mood Coach had been stuck in for what seemed like weeks.

Like his buddy Grant, Coach just couldn't get the question out of his head: Why did he coach? He thought to himself as he passed through the hills of Franklin County. Was it love of the game? The competition? The kids? Of course it was for the kids . . . right? That's why everyone coaches. It was obvious. He wanted them to be successful as players so they would eventually be successful in life—that was the reason he coached . . . or was it? Right now he was so frustrated with his players, he couldn't even think of them without turning to anger. How could they not care about winning as much as he did? He squeezed the steering wheel in frustration as he rolled to a stop against the curb of his parking spot behind the gym.

Once inside, he walked slowly down the long, lonely hallway to his office. Although he almost always seemed hurried, Coach appeared different today. He was really starting to drag, and since no one was around to see him, he didn't have to worry about trying to maintain his fast-paced, energetic image to anyone.

Settling into his desk chair, he noticed a familiar sound off in the distance, a sound he normally loved to hear, but for some reason, the sound wasn't appealing to him at all this morning. It was the sound of a basketball bouncing. He looked at the clock on the wall. *Ten till six . . . Hmm . . . I wonder who's shooting baskets at this hour?*

He got up from his desk and walked over to the entrance to the gym. As he stepped around the corner and looked onto the court, he saw, to his surprise, David Kelton, his star center. All alone, David was working on his post moves. Passing the ball to himself, he'd fake right, then go left; fake left, then go right. He did this over and over as Coach stood in the corner, watching without David's knowing he was there. After about five minutes, Coach walked onto the gym floor and greeted him.

"Morning, David," said Coach, making his way across the giant image of a Knight painted in the center of the court. "What brings you here so early?"

David put the ball down and wiped the sweat off his forehead with his T-shirt. "Workin' on my game, Coach. Tryin' to get better for the team . . . you know, like you tell us, Coach, 'Work harder . . . be a better player . . . a better leader. That's what I'm tryin' to do." David tried his best to catch his breath.

"Hey, that's great. Glad at least one of you has a little bit of heart left behind that jersey," Coach replied, unable to hide his frustration or sarcasm anymore. "Can I ask you something, David?"

"Sure, Coach. Shoot."

"Why do you play basketball?"

David picked the ball up and looked down at it for a moment before responding. "Well, I guess because it's fun . . .

or at least it *used* to be. I don't know. My dad was a great player, so since the age of five it was pretty much a given that this is what I'd be doing. That's probably part of the reason too. Of course, a scholarship is a pretty good reason, too . . . I guess." David started going through his drills again.

"Sure, those are all pretty good reasons," shot back Coach, "but what about the thrill of victory? Isn't that a big part of it? I don't understand how that isn't even *part* of the reason you play. I know it was a big part of the goals we all talked about at the beginning of the season." Coach was obviously trying to lay a guilt trip on his senior.

"Yeah . . . Of course I like to win. But for some reason, this year's been different. I can't really explain it, either." David's emotions began to escalate as he continued his drills. No doubt there was tension in the air, but David was determined to keep the majority of his feelings to himself.

"Well, all I know is that it seems kind of selfish for you to not be worried about winning as much as your teammates are, especially given that you're the leader of this team when it comes down to it," snapped Coach.

David, unable to resist some sarcasm of his own, fired back. "I know, Coach. It's all about our lack of leadership, and it starts with me. My fault, I know, and I'm working on it. I'm working on it—believe me."

"Well, hopefully the rest of us get to see the results of your work before the season's over, son. Like maybe tomorrow night?" Coach shook his head and turned to walk back to his office.

Out of the corner of his eye, he noticed Joe working on a light fixture by one of the side entrances to the gym. He quickly looked away, hoping to go unnoticed. Too late.

"Good morning, Coach!" Joe yelled across the gym. "Beautiful day out there, isn't it?"

"Don't know, Joe. It was dark and raining when I came in a half hour ago," replied Coach, continuing his walk toward the door.

"Who's to say dark and rainy isn't beautiful?" replied Joe.

Coach gave Joe a fake smile and halfhearted wave hoping to end the conversation as he headed out of the gym. "Have a good day, Joe."

Three-thirty, the normal starting time for practice, used to never come quick enough for Coach Rocker. However, over the last three weeks, the team's constant struggles had made practice something both Coach and his players dreaded more and more as the season wore on. But despite this, the day's practice had gone fairly well until the team started to scrimmage five-on-five. And then the wheels came off the bus.

First, the starters turned the ball over two times in a row. Coach remained calm, even though both turnovers were the result of stupid mistakes rather than good defense. Soon after that, the second team scored an easy lay-up on a simple backdoor play. Coach stood with his arms crossed using every muscle in his body to resist going ballistic, especially since it was the night before a big game. But then it happened: On another simple backdoor play, the defense broke down again and gave up an easy dunk. It was all he could take.

The shrill sound of Coach's whistle silenced the gym. "Stop! What the h— are we *thinking*? Do you guys have a *clue* what you're doing out here? Turnovers, defensive breakdowns—there's no focus, no one's stepping up. No one wants to get after it! Once again, no frickin' leadership! None! Do you hear me, *David, 6' 9" senior All-stater*!" Coach yelled sarcastically. "Do you hear me, seniors? Do any of you worthless bums hear me? I'm sick of it. Absolutely sick of it! You guys know better than me—you all do! You don't give a d— if we win another game or not!" Spit flew from his mouth as he screamed the words at his players. "You know what? You guys are just a bunch of self-centered losers. That's it, *losers*! And I've *had* it!"

He threw his clipboard into the bleachers and continued his rampage. "I haven't slept even *close* to a full night for over a month now. In all my years of coaching, I've never dealt with a group of guys this talented, and yet this selfish and lazy! You guys just don't get it!" Coach's face was beet red now as he paced the floor. "You know what I really wanna know? I wanna know why you guys are even here. Seriously, why do you play basketball if you don't care about your teammates, or working hard, or competing—or winning, for that matter. Why? *Why? Why!*"

He stopped and stared into the eyes of his players for what seemed an eternity. No one said a word. "You know what? Just get outta here!" The guys stood almost paralyzed, flashing looks at each other, scared to be the first to make a move. Then Coach said it again, even louder. "You heard me: *Get the h— out of here!* I'll see you at the game tomorrow night. And you better be ready to play!" Finished with his frenzied attack, Coach turned and stormed out of the gym toward his office as the rest of the team headed for the lockers.

Once inside his office, Coach slammed the door and sat down at his desk. Why was this happening to him? he wondered. What was the point of all his work? Was he losing it? Was the game passing him by? *No way*, he thought. He'd stared adversity in the face plenty of times before and had always been able to work his way out of it. But why was it that this time, for some reason, things seemed different?

A gentle tap at his door interrupted his thoughts. He assumed it was one of his assistants. "Door's open! Come in!" he yelled.

As the door slowly opened, Joe Taylor poked his head around the corner. "Excuse me, Coach, but . . . can I come in for just a second?"

Great, Coach thought. *Just what I need: A janitor telling me how to coach.* Feeling he had no other option, Coach reluctantly accepted the request. "Sure, Joe, what's up?"

"Well, I just wanted to encourage you, Coach, as a leader, a leader with an incredible opportunity. I know this season has been like none other you've ever experienced. But I know," said Joe, almost fatherly, "that you'll make it right in the end. Those kids need you to make it right, Coach. They need to see what it's all really about . . . you know, the *reason* they're here in the first place. The real heart of the matter." Joe paused for a moment and looked straight into Coach's eyes as he carefully chose his next words. "I know you'll get 'em there, Coach. Just don't give up." And with that, he turned and slowly walked out.

Coach sat in the company of his own thoughts long after Joe left. Once again, the *reason* was front and center. *They already know why they're here . . . I've told 'em a million times. They're just not getting it.* Confused as ever, he gathered his notes and the game film and headed home for the evening.

Chapter 6

Sharing Rock Bottom

In the midst of their struggles, the Knights were still expected to beat the Springston Tigers handily after pounding them by fourteen points in last season's home opener. No one was surprised when David Kelton's dunk near the end of the first quarter gave them a ten-point lead. It appeared the Knights were finally coming together as they continued to dominate, maintaining the double-digit lead throughout the first three quarters of the game. But then the momentum shifted.

Unwilling to go down without a fight, the Tigers began to press. Within the first two minutes of the fourth quarter, a deep three, a couple of quick steals, and two easy lay-ups cut the Knights' lead to just four points.

Finally, after getting the ball to Kelton the next three possessions, the Knights were able to at least maintain their four-point advantage as they exchanged baskets with the Tigers until the two-minute mark of the game. Then it happened: the Tigers' sharpshooter Jurell Swanson got open for a three-pointer off a double screen on the baseline and buried it, cutting the lead to only one point with just 1:30 showing on the clock.

The Knights answered by getting the ball inside to Kelton again and, although he was fouled, he knocked in both free throws, putting the lead back to three. Far from being done, the Tigers raced down the floor and began to work the ball around the perimeter. With just over thirty seconds left, Swanson again got open for a three that, after bouncing high off the back of the rim, took one more lucky bounce and settled through the bottom of the net to tie things up with just twenty-two seconds left to play. Coach Rocker called a timeout.

As the team jogged back to the huddle, the look on Coach's face told the story well. He couldn't believe they'd let the Tigers' best shooter get open for two three-pointers in the last minute and a half.

"Do you guys understand that Swanson can shoot the three?" Coach couldn't resist using sarcasm to make his point. "Does anybody want to play defense on this team? You guys are staring another loss square in the eyes, and apparently you don't give a rip!" He paused for effect. "I want you to wait until the ten second mark, then run *Wildcat 2* for David. Get him the ball, and David, you finish it!"

David was used to the pressure and typically wanted the ball in this situation; however, at this point, he was also stinging from Coach's comments. He could feel the pressure mounting, his heart pounding away in his chest. Sensing Coach was about to go over the edge, he felt a deep pang of fear shoot through his body at the thought of losing the game, of failing.

After inbounding the ball, Billy Conner, the Knights' senior point guard, calmly dribbled toward center court while being hawked by the Tigers' defense. Thirteen, twelve, eleven . . . Billy called out for *Wildcat 2* to start. The clock ticked— ten, nine, eight—as David came off of two hard screens and curled around toward the ball. Conner floated the pass into him. He caught it and began to square around to shoot. Out of nowhere, a Tiger defender deflected the ball, sending it right into Swanson's waiting hands at the top of the key.

Swanson turned and raced toward the other end of the floor as the clock showed three seconds . . . two seconds . . . one . . . He stopped four feet beyond the three-point arc to fire a shot of desperation. The ball floated toward the basket as the final buzzer sounded. The whole gym fell silent as Swanson's shot continued on its flight toward the rim. And then, without grazing a bit of iron, the ball swished, dead center, through the bottom of the net. There was instant pandemonium as the fans spilled onto the floor to celebrate the upset.

With his head buried in his hands, Coach sat in utter disbelief. This had to be a nightmare. He was just sure he would wake up, but when he raised his head from his hands, the scoreboard confirmed his worst fear: 73–70. Knights lose . . . again. What's worse, this was their fifth loss of the season and their third loss in the district. *This must be what people call "rock bottom,"* thought Coach as he walked over to shake the opposing coach's hand. *How can it get any worse?*

After briefly stopping in the hallway to gather his thoughts, Coach begrudgingly dragged himself into the locker room to face the team. As the door swung closed behind him he noticed the players all huddled around someone in the far corner. Something wasn't right. As Coach made his way toward the group, one by one the players dispersed. And then he saw it. To his utter disbelief, he saw David holding his right hand and crying in pain as the team trainers and a doctor tried to calm him down.

Upon entering the locker room following the game, David, in a fit of anger, had punched one of the lockers. Now he was dealing with the pain of what appeared to be a shattered hand.

As the trainer removed the blood-soaked towel, Coach stood horrified by the sight of his star senior's deformed hand. Unfortunately, he was even more horrified by the thought of losing him for the season. This would be a devastating blow to the team. *How could he do this? How could he be so selfish?* Coach thought as he resisted the urge to tear into him for his stupidity.

After sending David to the hospital with the team trainer, Coach sat on the bench in front of the team. For the first time in his twenty years as head coach, he was nearly speechless. Looking into his players' eyes, he could see their pain, but he still wondered why it felt like he hurt worse than they did.

"Guys, I got nothing to say right now. Just get dressed and get on the bus." Coach stood up and walked out without saying another word.

The bus ride back to Franklin North that night seemed endless. Coach received the call from the team doctor that confirmed David had broken three bones in his hand and would probably be out the rest of the season. So understandably, upon arriving at the school, he was still in no mood to talk. But given the situation, he knew he had to address the issue before sending the guys home for the weekend, so he stood up and faced the team.

"Don't really know what to say to you guys tonight," sighed Coach with an eerie calm in his voice. "David broke three bones in his hand. One bad decision, and just like that . . . his senior season is over. Guess if he doesn't have any more self-control than that, he gets what he deserves. It's just too bad you all have to pay the price for his selfishness, too." Coach grimaced as he rubbed his hand across the back of his neck, a habit he'd picked up from his dad, who used to do the same thing whenever he was frustrated.

"Regarding the game . . . once again boys, stupid mistakes and a lack of effort really hurt us. But, you know what? That wasn't what killed us. Nope. It was, once again, a lack of leadership. Seniors, I'm especially talking to you. No leadership from any of you. Again. I have no idea where you guys were tonight, but it was obvious you weren't here, at least during the fourth quarter, when it counted. I hate to sound like a broken record, but until you get it, I'll have to keep saying it: We've got to have some leadership on this team. Do you guys hear me? You have to learn to lead. If you ever want to win again—in fact, if you ever want to win in this life, you have to learn to *LEAD*, for God's sake! No practice tomorrow. Instead, I want you to take the weekend off and do some soul searching. I'll see you all back here on Monday." Coach turned, jumped down the steps of the bus, and with his head down, walked across the dimly lit parking lot to his car.

Saturday morning Coach woke up on the couch in his den feeling like he'd been run over by a Mack truck. He was still in his suit from the night before, and the TV was still on. He'd fallen asleep sometime around 3:00 a.m. while trying to break down game film. Now the smell of coffee in the kitchen was the only inspiration he had to get off the couch and begin the new day.

Coach walked through the living room, where Brandon was zoned into the TV screen as he played basketball on his Playstation. "Morning, Bud"; no response. Ticked off his son was ignoring him, he stopped in his tracks and tried again. "I said, 'Good morning, Bud!'"; still no response. Coach walked over in front of the TV. "Brandon!" he yelled, startling his son. "When I say good morning, I expect a response!"

"Okay, Dad . . . Geeesh . . . I didn't hear you."

Frustrated at the level of disrespect he felt, Coach briefly considered a lecture before deciding to let it go as his head still pounded from the night before.

"What's up with Brandon?" Coach asked as he walked into the kitchen, where Kathy and Kylee were enjoying breakfast together at the table.

"I don't know. Why do you ask?" replied Kathy.

"Well, first of all, he ignored me when I tried to say good morning to him. Then, when I finally got his attention, he shot off his mouth at me—not really like him."

Kathy, unable to resist the opportunity, shot back sarcastically, "Well, for starters, he's been playing a lot more of his video games. I think he's kinda drowning himself in them. Of course, if you'd ever spend any *time* with him, you might have a better idea of what he's struggling with."

This was clearly a low blow from his wife filled with tensions that had been building for months. "Hey, will you give me a break? I'm doing the best I know how right now with all that's going on with the team, and now losing David. Come on, Kathy, lay off."

"Right, Steve. I gotcha. Sorry, I didn't mean to interrupt your life with issues from your family."

Although Coach's first reaction was to let her have it for her insensitivity, he noticed Kylee was now listening intently to the exchange taking place between her parents. He took a deep breath to gather himself, then, without saying a word, he finished pouring his cup of coffee and, shaking his head, walked back to the den.

As he settled into his leather recliner to read the Saturday morning paper, his cell phone buzzed. The name flashed across the tiny screen: Grant Steffin. "Hey, Grant, what's up?" Coach answered in a dejected tone.

"Morning, Steve. Another tough one last night, huh?"

"Yeah, and you don't know the half of it. Kelton punched a locker after the game and pretty much shattered his hand. Done for the season. How stupid is that? Why do none of these kids have any self-control? Lazy, selfish, and now stupid, too? Not a lot for us to look forward to with the upcoming generation, huh? You can pretty much stick a fork in our season. In fact, probably my job, too."

For a couple of seconds Grant was silent on the other end of the line, not really knowing what to say. Then, in an attempt at empathy, he spoke again. "That really sucks, Steve. Listen, why don't you come by around noon today? I'll grill us a couple burgers and we can cry in our beer together."

Coach thought for a minute, then remembered Kathy was planning on taking the kids to the zoo for the day. *Perfect,* he thought to himself. He could go and not feel guilty. "Sure, see you around noon," Coach agreed, then closed his phone.

The sound of the waterfall splashing into the pool had a soothing effect on Coach as he sat waiting for Grant to return with the cold drinks.

"So we know *my* life is a wreck right now. How are you doing, Grant?" Coach asked, hoping to talk about something other than his own troubles for a while.

"Well, to tell you the truth, I think it's kind of ironic that we're really in similar spots right now. I mean, I'm up against the wall at work. Our turnover's going through the roof. I've lost two of my top executives in just the last four weeks. One

I fired for insubordination, as an example for the rest of the team. Then a week later his buddy, our top sales executive, resigned." Grant shook his head in frustration. "The board is really breathing down my neck. And the people . . . the people still just don't get it. We continue to deal with issues resulting from a workforce that just doesn't seem to care."

Grant paused to take a swig of his beer, then with a blank stare on his face fixed his eyes on the water falling into the pool. "And as for me personally, I'm . . . well, I guess I'm flat-out miserable. Which doesn't really make much sense to me, since I typically thrive under this type of pressure. I mean, I have a busier schedule than ever before in my life. I have more money, more people around me, and more things than I'd ever imagined in my wildest dreams I'd have. And yet, I feel more alone now than ever before in my life." He paused again as the blank stare seemed to deepen.

"Michael called me last week, crying. Said his mom told him I didn't care about him anymore. She said my work was my family. Why would she do that to him? He doesn't deserve to hear that kind of crap." Grant's eyes began to well up with tears as he struggled at the thought of his son's hurt. "I have to figure this thing out. I have to figure out how to get this company back on track so I can get my life back in order."

After a few uncomfortably quiet moments, Grant stood up and walked over to the grill to put the burgers on.

"Ya know, Grant, we really are dealing with a lot of the same struggles right now. You ever think God looks down on us and purposefully does stuff like this?"

"Like what?" Grant asked.

"Well . . . I mean, like put certain people together at certain times. You know, so they can share in each other's pain?"

"Who knows?" said Grant, the majority of his attention shifting to the burgers he was grilling.

Coach stood up now, too, as if the proverbial light bulb had lit up in his head. "Or maybe it's more so they can help each other find the answers to the tough questions that always come up during tough times. Maybe we're not supposed to figure everything out on our own. Maybe we actually need others to help us—to help us find our way through the mess."

"Who knows?" said Grant. "I know I've been dealing with a ton of questions rolling around in my head lately. Can't seem to get any of 'em answered on my own, either. But in my shoes, you know, at the top, I don't have a choice. I have to find the answers on my own because most others I talk to have some sort of hidden agenda in the back of their minds. Instead of being candid with me, they tell me what they think I want to hear—either out of fear of losing their job, or money, or having a 'powerful connection,' or . . . or out of their desire for more: more money, a promotion, more power, or whatever."

"Huh," interrupted Coach. "Sounds a lot like the hatchet-treasure thing again to me."

Grant considered the thought for a moment. "Yeah, ya know . . . I guess it is. When it comes right down to it, people are still pretty much only motivated by those two things," Grant said, "especially in those superficial relationships."

Flames shot out of the grill as Grant quickly turned his attention back to the burgers. "Whoa! Looks like these babies are ready for eatin'."

"You know," said Coach, "that's why our jobs become so much more challenging in tough times. 'Cause in the past, we could always rely on dollars or wins to be the primary method of motivation we used, followed closely by the threat of punishment here and there if someone stepped out of line. Unfortunately, at least with me, I can't seem to *buy* a win right now. And the hatchet—the threats I've been using just aren't working, either. It feels like I'm heading into a downward spiral and can't stop." Coach turned his attention to the juicy cheeseburger Grant had just handed him and took his first big bite.

"Yep . . . wish I had an answer for that one, 'cause I feel your pain," said Grant as he stuffed a bite of his own burger into his mouth. "Seems like about the time you do feel like you have the downward spiral stopped, you lose a key person and have to start all over again." Grant, noticing his friend had finished his drink, set his plate down and headed toward the sliding door of the house to grab some more beers.

As he sat by the pool waiting quietly for Grant to return, Coach listened to the peaceful sounds of the waterfall splashing into the pool in the background. *There just has to be more to it,* he thought. He felt horrible for all that Grant was going through, especially with his family, and yet he feared that he himself might be heading down a similar path. What were they missing? He had to figure this thing out. Some way, somehow, he was determined to get to the heart of the issue.

Chapter 7

Mondays with Joe

U nable to sleep Monday morning, Coach rolled out of bed and got an early start to the week by heading into school around 4:30 a.m. As he pulled into his normal parking spot just before 5:00, he noticed the light on in Joe's office. *Wow*, he thought, *I knew Joe got here early, but I had no idea this early. Wonder what he does at this hour?* His curiosity was more than he could stand, so instead of heading straight to his own office, he took the long way around to swing by Joe's first.

Although he'd never been in Joe's office, he had a pretty clear picture of what a janitor's office might look like. He pictured tools and cleaning supplies strewn about. Maybe a poster of a muscle car or two on the wall—the usual things janitors might be interested in. But as he walked softly up to the door, which was halfway open, he saw something completely different from what he'd ever expected.

Floor-to-ceiling bookshelves lined two of the walls and were filled with every kind of book you could imagine. Classic literature, business books, biographies, leadership books: you name it, he had it. Hundreds of them, all neatly organized. Of course, Joe's trusty toolbox sat off in the corner, but other than that, there was little evidence of this being a janitor's office.

"Good morning, Coach!" Joe said from a worn-out reading chair in the corner of the room. "Beautiful day out there, isn't it?"

"Sure . . . I guess. Still a little dark yet, but if you say so," answered Coach, continuing to scan the room in amazement. There were pictures everywhere: pictures of what appeared to be Joe's family, pictures of students posing with Joe smiling and waving, pictures of students with notes signed to Joe, even some pictures of a couple of former Franklin students as college athletes, autographed to Joe. It was obvious by the sheer number of pictures that he was a pretty popular figure at Franklin North.

"Come on in, Coach. Sit down. I was just thinking about you," said Joe. "Can I get you a cup of 'joe'?" He winked and smirked at his pun.

Coach chuckled. "Sure, why not?"

"You're here pretty early, aren't you?" asked Joe, an inquisitive look in his eye.

"Couldn't sleep this morning. Too much going on right now, I guess. I gotta get this team back on track, you know, before it's too late. And with Kelton out for the season, it might already be too late."

Joe looked at Coach sympathetically. "Hmm . . . too late. Too late for what, Coach?" Joe asked, pouring two cups of coffee from the old coffee pot stationed behind his desk.

"You know, too late to salvage the season. Remember, we were preseason number one in the state . . . a pretty good bet to win it all. Now it looks like we'll be lucky to get out of our district, let alone win state. This whole season has been one huge failure so far. And if I don't change something fast, the rest of the season'll be that way, too," Coach said, looking at his watch as if suddenly in a rush.

"Why do you think this season's been such a failure?" asked Joe, taking a sip of the steaming hot brew in his cup.

"I think it's pretty obvious. When it comes right down to it, we're expected to be winning, and we're not. Plain and simple, the kids just don't want to win bad enough. They just don't seem to really care anymore. And as much as I've tried to change their attitude, they still don't get it."

"Get what?" Joe asked, again as if he really were lost.

"Get that it takes hard work to achieve your goals, that you have to be willing to sacrifice for your teammates. You know, that you can't be selfish. Even the senior leaders on our team don't get it. All they're concerned about is what's important to them: points, rebounds . . . stats. Never mind what's important to the team," said Coach, frustration growing on his face.

"So what *should* be important to the team?" asked Joe.

"Winning . . . Uh . . ." Coach caught himself and knew he needed to back up to explain. "Well, early in the season, anyway, we set goals as a team. The players wanted to win the district, the region, and, of course, the state. So, you know, I guess that's what's important to the team, but just not the individuals."

"But isn't the team made up of the individuals?" asked Joe.

"Yeah . . . I guess that's what's been such a big disappointment right now. Before the season we all agreed that this is what we wanted to accomplish as a team, and now it seems they don't care about that anymore."

"If you don't mind my asking, why is that, Coach? I mean, why don't they seem to care?" asked Joe.

"I don't have a clue. That's what I've been trying to figure out for the past month. I've tried everything. Once we started losing, it was like everything went out the window. They got lazy, complacent; you know, content with mediocrity. They coasted, and nothing I could do or say would change it. Winning just wasn't important enough to them any-more. I guess they'd won too much already. Then, I tried to get tougher on 'em. I begged, yelled, screamed, threw things, even kicked 'em out of practice."

"Did it work?" asked Joe, sitting on the edge of his seat, attentively listening.

"Nothing seems to work. These kids just don't give a rip anymore—period. Then, of course, to top it all off, my senior star goes off in the locker room after the last game and ends up breaking his hand, ending his high school career. Talk about selfish! Never thought about the effect his lack of self-control might have on his teammates, did he?"

"My, my, Coach, it sounds like you have your hands full, like your back's really against the wall."

"Yeah. That sums it up pretty well."

"How's your family doing?" asked Joe.

"Uh . . . fine, I guess. You know, they understand the pres-sure I'm facing right now, so they've pretty much learned to stay clear."

"I see," said Joe, a look of sadness in his eyes. "So I'm curi-ous: what's your plan?"

"Whaddya mean, what's my plan?"

"Well, you said earlier that you needed to change some-thing fast in order to salvage the season. That *is* what you said, right?" asked Joe.

"Yeah . . . I guess so," Coach answered with a bewildered look on his face.

"Well, what's your plan to change it?" asked Joe, a bit more authority in his voice.

"I . . . I guess I don't know yet. I mean, here's the thing. When it comes right down to it, most people are motivated by two main things: reward and fear. Translated into basketball terms, that means wins or losses. Our team won so much last year and had so much success that they've kinda lost their motivation to win."

"Okay, I think I understand. So if what you say is true, then the fear of losing should help them overcome their lack of motivation to win . . . right?" Joe seemed a bit skeptical of the thought.

"Well, yeah, but—"

"So why are you still losing?"

"Well, there's more to the wins and losses thing. You see, it's kinda like . . . Well, do you know Grant Steffin of Cybelcom?"

"Of course I know of him."

"Well, Grant's a good friend of mine, and he's been struggling with a lot of similar things at work. He has this theory . . . about a hatchet and treasure." Coach stood up and walked over to the whiteboard hanging behind Joe's desk. "Can I use this?" Coach asked, wondering why Joe had one of these in his office in the first place.

"Be my guest," Joe said.

In the middle of the whiteboard, Coach drew the best stick figure he knew how. Then, imitating Grant, he drew what looked like a coin with a dollar sign over the left hand and a hatchet over the right. "You see, this is it, Joe. This is what leadership is all about. If you want to get someone to do something, you have to be able to wield one of these two things in front of 'em at all times. You pay 'em well or you punish 'em hard. Just depends on the situation at hand."

Joe rubbed his chin. "So tell me again, how does that relate to what you're dealing with now with your players?"

"Well, like I said, winning is our treasure in sports. It's like the dollar in business." Coach wrote a W above the dollar sign on the board. "And I think my guys have won so much in the past that they've lost the motivation to win anymore."

"Yeah," said Joe, concerned.

"So now—now my only choice is to bring out the hatchet. You know, to increase the fear of losing proportionately, so that they eventually become more inspired to win again. I have to make their lives hell when they lose. That's the only way out right now . . ."

Coach's voice trailed off as he recognized the predicament. He knew all too well how this concept had been failing in the past two weeks, but he was convinced this was the only option he had.

Joe sat silently and stared at the picture Coach had drawn on his whiteboard. "Quite a challenge you have ahead of yourself, Coach," Joe said, breaking what seemed like an eternity of silence. "But looks like you know the reason these kids do what they do, so now all you have to do is get your philosophy to work. You know, get 'em to want to win bad enough again to actually be willing to sacrifice for one another. And just because it hasn't worked yet doesn't mean it won't eventually work, right? After all, I'm sure it's worked in past years. You have to stick to your guns. Or should I say your hatchets?"

Joe was such an encourager that it was hard for Coach to tell whether he was serious or was challenging him to question his philosophy a little more deeply. He knew that both the treasure and the hatchet were losing their effectiveness, but he also could think of no other alternative. He had to make it work one way or another.

Just then there was a knock at Joe's door, followed by a

young man's voice from the hall. "Mr. Taylor . . . are you busy? I can come back . . ." Joe glanced at the clock on the wall.

"Gosh, I had no idea it was already 6:15," Joe said under his breath. "No, no, Marcus, come on in; we're just finishing up." Joe walked over to the door and greeted Marcus with a hug.

"Coach, you know Marcus Williams, don't you?"

"Uh, yeah," said Coach, half embarrassed that he only knew him by name but had never officially met him.

Marcus was a senior running back at Franklin North who had already committed to the University of Notre Dame, where he planned to play football and study law. His was one of those incredible stories of a kid coming from one of the poorest neighborhoods of Franklin and making something of himself. From the first day of school, he was in trouble, fighting, skipping class, cheating, to name just a few of the things that put him at risk of being permanently expelled. But then things started to change.

Somehow Marcus had turned it all around and, after realizing the true potential he had, both in the classroom and on the field, he had become a student nearly everyone looked up to.

"You sure you don't want me to come back later, Mr. Taylor?" Marcus asked politely.

"No, we had a meeting scheduled for 6:15, right?"

"Yeah, but I understand if—"

"Marcus—" Joe interrupted and spoke sternly now—"we always keep our commitments, right?"

"Yes, sir," Marcus replied respectfully.

"Okay, then. Coach Rocker and I were just finishing up,

so come on in." Coach headed toward the door as Joe followed him into the hallway.

"Coach, I really enjoyed our chat this morning, and I'm sorry if it got cut short. But I truly hope you figure this thing out soon. You know, a lot of folks are counting on you . . . including your family." Joe extended his hand to Coach, then, as he looked into his eyes with genuine compassion, he patted him on the shoulder and said, "Stop by anytime, Coach. Let me know how things are going, okay?" And with that, Joe headed back into his office.

Coach made his way back to his office utterly confused at what he'd just experienced. What was it about Joe Taylor that made him so intriguing? How did he seem to know so much about so much? And why did the kids all flock to him? Even Marcus Williams, the proverbial "big man on campus," was drawn to him. *He's a janitor, for God's sake!* he thought to himself.

Whatever it was about Joe, whatever he had, it was starting to get to Coach, too. In fact, Coach made up his mind right then and there that he was going to pop in on Joe again in a couple of days to try to continue their conversation about the hatchet and the treasure. For some reason, he sensed Joe could help.

Chapter 8

The Ride Continues

The next few practices were relatively normal. However, with a record of 5–5, Coach was still on edge and would go nuts at the slightest hint of selfishness or laziness from the team. Although he occasionally saw hints of improvement, defensively the guys were still struggling, especially without Kelton in the middle to bail them out when there was a breakdown on the perimeter. As patient as Coach tried to be, he knew Friday's game presented a must-win situation. So as the week wore on, he felt he had no choice but to push his players to the very edge of what they could take. And he did. He was convinced they had to fear losing this week, big time!

Shortly after Thursday's practice, Brant Stevens, the Knights' small forward, sheepishly peeked his head through the doorway of Coach's office.

"What's up, Brant?" asked Coach in a tone that politely hinted he felt interrupted and was in a hurry.

"Coach, I'll try to make this quick." Brant's voice quivered as he walked into the office and stood in front of his Coach's large, gray desk. Coach, busy answering e-mails, barely looked up at Brant. "I've thought hard about this for the past four weeks, Coach . . . and although this is difficult for me to say, I . . . I've decided to quit the team. And I want you to know that I've never quit anything in my entire life. But . . . but with what I'm facing at home right now, along with trying to keep my grades up, I feel it's best for myself, my family, and for my teammates."

Coach immediately stopped typing, looked up at Brant with a look of astonishment, and pushed back in his chair. He could hardly believe what he was hearing. Brant was the only junior starter on the team. And although he was a pretty quiet kid, he was a very good leader on the floor and almost always did what he was supposed to do.

"So that's it—things are getting a little tough on you, and you decide to quit?" Coach said, his voice shifting from frustration to anger.

"Like I said, Coach, I really—"

"Well, I guess if you don't care about your teammates anymore . . ."

Brant tried again to respond. "I do care about my teammates! It's just that . . . that—"

"That what? You can't take the heat, right? Just like every other selfish sissy on this team, things get tough and you want to bail out, right? Is that it?"

Brant stood motionless in front of his coach as if in shock. "You know what, Coach? I—"

Coach fired back again. "No, I don't know what, and I really don't care either, Brant. All I know is that you're making a selfish decision. You're letting your team down, so turn in your gear and *get out*! I have no use for quitters, so this conversation is over."

With a look of both disbelief and dejection, Brant turned and walked out. He knew his coach was under a lot of pressure, but he couldn't believe he wouldn't even listen to his reasoning. As he walked back toward the locker room, tears rolled down the side of his cheeks. He thought about his teammates and all the great times he'd had with them now coming to an end. Still, as he thought more about it, he felt a sense of relief come over him as the interaction, in many ways, confirmed where his coach's heart really was in the first place. So with that, Brant cleaned out his locker and slowly walked out of the empty locker room for what he knew would be his last time ever.

Back in his office Coach, still steaming over the interaction, wrestled with his thoughts. What was going on? This season was becoming a nightmare. Where had he gone wrong? It seemed everything he'd worked so hard to accomplish was now crumbling before his eyes. His past successes were becoming less and less meaningful as his current failures cast a dark shadow over them, both in his eyes and in the public's. And now, with his star center out for good and his best junior off the team, any hopes of salvaging the season were all but lost. *Success will have to wait for another time . . . and another place,* he thought as he stared at past championship pictures hanging on the wall of his office.

What's wrong with these kids? How are they all so messed up? He muttered to himself as he shut down his computer and gathered his stuff to head home for the evening.

Despite his expectations for a disaster, Friday night's game against East Side went relatively well. After a slow start, the Knights heated up from the outside and took the lead midway through the second quarter. Much to Coach's surprise, the guys played hard and executed both offensively and defensively throughout most of the game. In the end, the Knights had outplayed the Bulldogs on both ends of the floor, giving the

Knights a 62–54 victory at a key point in the season and bringing their record to a still-disappointing 6–5.

Unfortunately, the joy that victory usually brings a team was cut short by Coach's locker room speech after the game. He complimented the guys for finally playing together, but then, out of fear that they would become too satisfied with where they were, he blasted them regarding their shortcomings. He knew he had to continue to pound them about their usual lack of leadership and selfishness if they were ever to really get back on the winning track.

"If you guys'll recall, this season wasn't about beating the Bulldogs, and it wasn't originally about having a winning record either, especially 6–5." Coach shook his head and rolled his eyes at the thought of such mediocrity. "All year we've talked about leadership and how you've all been selfish—focused on your own things instead of the team. And as a result, this is where we are: sitting 3–3 in our district, unranked in the state, and without two of our original starters. Is that success? Are you guys happy with where you are today? I sure hope not, because I know *I'm* not. In fact, I get sick to my stomach just thinking about how great you guys coulda been this season. And yet here we are, a true picture of underachievement."

Coach paced back and forth in front of the team as he talked. "When you go home tonight, I want you all to think about that and consider the role you played in it. Next, think about what you'll do next week to change it, because one win does not a season make, my friends. I know I'm not satisfied, and you better not be either!" He paused and scanned the room, hoping to see a spark of emotion in his players' eyes.

Nothing. "I'll see you all on Monday." He bent down, picked up his notes, and walked out of the locker room.

Why am I feeling so miserable after a win? he thought as he walked into his office. In an instant his thoughts went to Grant's hatchet-treasure concept again. *Okay, Coach, you won a game . . . why does it feel like you lost? Maybe your treasure isn't working so well anymore either . . .* Confused and spent, his mind shifted gears. *Oh well. Hopefully the speech made the message loud and clear. We're here to win a lot more than just one game.*

Sunday morning came around and, as Kathy and the kids got ready for church, Coach sat in front of the TV watching the game tape with his remote control in hand. He was still taking notes on Friday night's game. Despite that it was a win, he'd watched the tape no fewer than five times, but he still felt he needed to study it more to determine what was wrong with his team. Kylee had just wandered into the room and hopped on the couch by her dad when Kathy popped her head around the corner.

"You coming to church with us today?" she asked, already guessing the answer.

"Not today, Kathy. Too much to do."

Kathy pressed the issue. "Steve, your kids would really enjoy some time with you today. And joining us for church would be a great start."

"Yeah, Daddy! Why don't ya join us?" chimed in Kylee, looking at her dad with her best puppy-dog eyes.

Coach looked over at his daughter. "Honey, Daddy really needs to get this right. Maybe we can spend some time together later this afternoon?"

Kathy, her hands on her hips, shook her head at her husband, knowing all too well what the chances of that were.

"How 'bout you guys go get some good news and bring it back for me, okay?" said Coach cynically.

Kathy rolled her eyes. "Come on, Kylee. Your *dad's* busy now." Kylee looked pleadingly at her dad one more time, but finding this had no effect, she got up and followed her mom out of the room.

Coach was left alone with his thoughts, and he fell into reminiscing. He had grown up going to church but had lost interest during his college days as he began to realize more and more he could never live up to the high expectations set by his church. Don't drink, don't fight, don't smoke, don't do drugs, don't steal, don't hate, don't cuss, don't have sex—and make sure you go to church every Sunday. It seemed like the list was endless. To him religion was nothing more than rules and rituals. On top of that, his parents practically beat the rules into his head, shaming him every time he did anything wrong by telling him that God was watching and would punish him if he stepped out of line. Finally, after failing over and over to live up to the expectations, Coach became bitter toward religion, his church, and even his parents for setting such stringent laws. Eventually, he gave up on the whole thing. He still believed in God and thought it was probably a good thing for his family to go to church; but for him, he just wasn't ready to try to live up to all those standards again. Especially at this point in his life. *That's all I need,* he thought. *To be reminded of more of my failings.*

Of course his views toward church weren't helped much when he watched his older brother Tim go off what he considered "the deep end" of religion. Tim and his family were always in church. Sunday morning, Sunday night, Wednesday night—when the church doors were open, Tim was there. Not only was he there, he was involved with everything. He was in the choir, served as a deacon, headed up the church's mission board. He practically lived at the church.

But one day, it all came crashing down. Tim's wife, Kristen, packed her bags and ran away with another guy. She said she was tired . . . couldn't take it anymore. Coach couldn't really blame her; Tim was married to the church, spending every waking hour on "the Lord's work" while his own family fell apart. They eventually divorced, and Tim left the church altogether. He pretty much gave up his religion after that. *All that time, Tim thought if he did all those things, God would bless him. You know, with money, and health, and all the things those famous pastors tell you you'll get if you just give everything to the church. And yet all it got him was a broken family and a lonely life. So much for blessings,* thought Coach.

The bottom line was this: Coach saw no need for religion in his life. If rules and rewards were what God was all about, with all due respect, he'd work on it later on. For now, he had more important things to focus on.

Chapter 9

From the Inside Out

With thoughts of the upcoming week racing through his mind, Coach woke at 4:15 Monday morning and couldn't go back to sleep. Rather than waste time tossing and turning, he decided to get a jump on the week. Friday's win, his lack of contentment following the win, and the loss of Brant were still boggling his mind. Coach was determined to find some answers. And for some strange reason, he thought Joe Taylor just might know where he should start looking.

Coach pulled his car into his normal parking spot around 5:00 a.m. and breathed a sigh of relief when he noticed that the lights in Joe's office were already on. After struggling to find the right key to the gym, Coach unlocked the back door and walked quietly down the dark hallway toward the light coming from the half-opened doorway to Joe's office. He walked up to the door to peek inside. At first he didn't see Joe and wondered if maybe he was already off somewhere in the school fixing something. But when he poked his head in further, he found Joe sitting off in the corner, deeply engrossed in whatever it was he was reading.

"Joe," Coach said softly, trying not to startle him.

"Hey, Coach, how are ya?" answered Joe in his normal calm and caring manner.

"Pretty good . . . I guess. Is this a bad time?"

"Never a bad time for a cup of joe with a friend," replied Joe as he winked. He stood up and motioned for Coach to come in and sit down. "I was just doing a little brush-up reading on one of my favorite leaders."

"I see," said Coach, almost afraid to ask who his favorite leader was. "You have quite a collection of books, Joe. You must enjoy reading a lot."

"Not so much the reading part as the learning and growing part," said Joe, chuckling, as he walked over to the coffee pot and poured a cup for Coach. "Ya know, I learned a long time ago that the two things that most impact our lives are the people we spend our time with and the things we read. Yep. Relationships and reading." Joe paused as he set the cup down on the table beside Coach and then turned to walk back to his chair. "Ya know . . . come to think about it, God must have thought those two things were pretty important, too. I mean, given the way he set us up to grow as a result of both of those things in our lives, too. Go figure."

Sipping his coffee, Coach tried to figure out what Joe meant by his statement. "That's true . . . I guess. Well, I guess I don't really know, I mean . . . well . . . I guess I've never thought of it like that before." Coach fumbled with his words a bit. He hadn't expected to have a conversation about God with Joe, especially not this early in the morning.

Joe politely reassured Coach. "Oh, don't worry about it. Most folks don't think about it. They don't think about it *much,* anyway. So tell me, Coach, how are the boys doin'? Are you making any progress with 'em, you know, with that hatchet-treasure thing you've been working on?"

Coach squirmed in his chair. "Well, to tell you the truth, that's kinda what I was hoping to talk with you about this morning. I mean, the whole thing is really getting a bit confusing to me at this point."

"Whaddya mean when you say confusing, Coach?" asked Joe, resting his arms on the worn-out armrests of his chair.

"Well, Friday night we won, and for some reason, after the game I felt miserable. I mean, it didn't really mean anything to me. It was almost as if winning—my 'treasure'—wasn't motivating to *me* anymore . . ." Coach trailed off, discouraged.

"So you don't want to win this coming Friday?" asked Joe.

"Of course I do—in the worst way. I spent probably fifteen hours this weekend breaking down film."

"It sounds like winning still motivates you. So . . . I guess I don't understand what you're confused about," Joe said, tilting his head as if a bit confused now himself.

After pausing to think about what he was saying, Coach tried to clarify things. "I guess maybe I'm more frustrated than confused. I just don't understand why it seems like nothing's really worked this year. When Grant and I started talking about the hatchet and the treasure back at the beginning of the season, it all made perfect sense to me. I could really relate, and I felt like I'd found the answer to the problems we were dealing with."

Coach stood up and walked over to the whiteboard and pointed to the drawing still there from the week before. "The players had become too used to winning, so when winning lost its motivating power—" he pointed to the W sign on the stick man's left hand—"I had to compensate by instilling fear." Now he pointed to the hatchet on the stick man's right hand. "I yelled, I screamed, I threw things, I ran them until they puked. I even kicked 'em out of practice. And it worked, for a while. But eventually, that seemed to wear off, too. Guys started fighting more in practice. They fell apart in a couple of the games that followed. Then the unthinkable happened: David lost control in the locker room and cost himself the rest of his high school career. Finally, just when I think we may have stabilized, Brant quits, right in the middle of the season. I just don't get it. I must be missing something! I mean, like I said, Friday night I was miserable, and even after we'd won!"

Joe sat silently and looked at Coach with sympathy in his eyes. Finally, after what seemed like an hour of silence, he stood up and walked over to the whiteboard.

"Coach, can I ask you a question?"

Coach headed back to his seat. "Sure. Why not? Lord knows I won't have the answer, though."

Joe stood and stared at the drawing of the stick figure. "You see anything missing from this picture?"

"Other than skillful artistry, no. I think it's a pretty complete picture," snapped Coach.

"Well, let's think of it another way then. Besides the obvious answer of *leadership,* what's missing with your guys right now?"

Coach thought for a few seconds, then answered, "They don't care about winning anymore?"

"Okay, so they're missing the *will* to win, right?"

"Yeah, that's accurate," answered Coach.

Joe wrote the word WILL on the board. "What else are they missing?" asked Joe, determined to dig deeper now.

"Well, they don't care about their teammates," said Coach.

"Okay, so they're missing *love* for their teammates."

Coach jumped in. "Whoa . . . Love's a little strong, Joe, don't ya think? I mean these are high school guys we're talking about."

"Yeah," replied Joe. "So do you want guys that *like* the game or *love* the game?" Joe looked over his eyeglasses at Coach waiting for a response.

"Love, of course," Coach replied.

"Okay, you want guys who *like* to compete or *love* to compete?" pressed Joe, sharpening his point further.

"Okay, okay," replied Coach, throwing both hands in the air. "I get your point. Love's fine." Joe wrote the word LOVE on the board under the word WILL and then turned back to Coach.

"All right, anything else?" Joe was obviously fishing for something more.

"Well . . . I guess the only other word that comes to my mind when I watch them play is passion. They've really lost their passion for the game. And it shows—big time."

"Great!" said Joe, writing the word PASSION on the board.

"Whaddya mean, 'great'?" asked Coach defensively.

"No, no. Not great that they've lost their passion; I mean great that you've figured out three key things they're missing."

Joe walked back over to his seat and sat down. "Now look back at the stick figure on the board. Tell me, Coach, if you were a player on a basketball team missing those three things— will, love, and passion—and this was your coach, which hand do you think would best help you find them again?"

Coach looked at the picture in silence. Then hesitantly he took a stab at answering the question. "I guess . . . the treasure hand?"

"Remember," said Joe, "you've lost your will to win. That means that for some reason, you really don't care about winning anymore. And the treasure is equivalent to winning—that's your treasure, remember? So, how will more winning help you find your will to win again?" asked Joe.

"Guess it probably won't," answered Coach. "So I had a fifty-fifty chance of getting it right, and I missed it. Pretty true to form for me this year. Guess it must be the hatchet hand."

"Really? You sure?" asked Joe. Coach shrugged his shoulders as if to say he wasn't sure of anything anymore. "Let's say your son has lost his will to clean his room—if he ever had it in the first place. You tell him that if he doesn't clean it, he'll lose his Playstation privileges. Will he get his *will* to clean the room back?"

"Of course. In a heartbeat," said Coach confidently.

"No, not really," Joe said in a corrective manner. "You see, he'll clean it all right, but he'll clean it only because he still has his will to play Playstation, not because he regained his will to clean his room. Truth be known, over time he might begin to hate cleaning his room even more because not only is he doing something against his will, but what he is doing now has the potential to cause him even more pain by making him lose something he *does* have the will for." Joe paused for a few seconds to let the concept sink in before taking it a step further.

"What do you suppose will happen with the room when you're gone for a couple of days, Coach? Think he'll clean it?" Joe raised his eyebrows waiting for an answer.

"Not likely," answered Coach, knowing Brandon well.

"But when he knows you're coming home—and bringing your 'hatchet' with you—he'll clean it up in a flash, won't he?" Coach nodded in reassuring agreement.

"Don't misunderstand me, Coach. Punishment, discipline, is not a bad thing. But if it's the *only* thing, or even the *main* thing, it will eventually do more harm than good. Think about this: If the hatchet is the only method you use to motivate your son to clean his room, how do you think he'll feel about cleaning his room, say, ten years from now?"

"He'll hate it . . . really resent it," Coach said, as if he'd experienced this at some point in his life himself.

"So, how do you think he'll feel about the person who held the 'hatchet' for all those years?"

Coach sat silently for a moment as if things were beginning to sink in. "Probably pretty bad. Maybe even bitter or angry," he replied before leaning back in his chair and crossing his arms. "Okay, I think I get your point, but what other options are there? I mean, at some point you have to use the hatchet to get things done."

"Oh yes, I know. And in fact, I agree. The hatchet definitely has its place in all of our lives. But if someone has lost their *will* to do something, a hatchet, though it might work in the short-term, just won't work over the long haul, especially when it's used exclusively."

Joe walked over to the coffee pot, picked it up, and brought it back over to Coach to refill his cup. Once both cups were again brimming with hot coffee, he set the pot back down and stood by the whiteboard. He pointed to the word LOVE. "Let's look at the next thing the guys have lost: love for their teammates. But before digging into this one, let's clarify what the term love means in the first place, because our culture typically messes this one up." Joe walked back over to his chair and sat down.

"Personally, I like to look to Jesus as the ultimate example of what love is supposed to be. What are some of the first things that come to your mind when you think about the character of Jesus?"

"Wise, patient, compassionate," replied Coach. "He seemed to always be concerned about those less fortunate, or those who were hurting."

"Excellent!" said Joe. "*Why* was he compassionate?"

"Because he cared about people?" answered Coach with only a hint of confidence.

"Right. But let me ask you this: Did he already have a personal relationship with all those people . . . you know, like the blind men he healed, or the woman at the well, or the 5,000 people he fed? I mean, had they already spent time together and really got to know each other and then, in so doing, decided whether or not they liked each other?"

"Not that I'm aware of," answered Coach.

"You're right, but he still had compassion for all of them— meaning he felt bad they were hurting and had a desire to alleviate their pain. The great thing about Jesus' example to us is that he always acted on that desire. This is where we usually miss it with the compassion part of love in our society. We feel bad for someone, but we end up dropping the ball when it comes to doing something about it—the action part. Jesus, on the other hand, was the ultimate example of love. He always made the choice to *act*. And *that* is what lies at the core of the love he teaches us to have for one another: the *choice*."

Coach, with a perplexed look on his face, shifted in his chair. "I'm not sure I completely understand how the choice to act lies at the core of love. I guess I always kind of thought love was based more on feelings than actions."

"Don't feel bad, Coach. Most folks think that way. And that's one of the reasons we see so many broken relationships around us today. People think as soon as the *feeling* of love stops, love stops. And it shouldn't!

"Fact is, the love Jesus exemplified was not about a feeling, or an attraction, for that matter. Like I said, it was a decision—a *choice*. A choice to act that was not dependent upon certain conditions being met. No matter what the situation was, Jesus chose to love, and he showed it through his every action." Joe looked at Coach intently, hoping to get a feel for his level of understanding.

"So the love that my guys have lost . . . really comes down to a choice?" asked Coach hesitantly.

"In essence, yes. Basically, they're choosing not to love their teammates for reasons of their own. It may be frustration, selfishness, or just plain old personality clashes, but for whatever reasons, they're choosing not to love one another."

Coach pursed his lips and sighed as he considered the truth Joe had just revealed to him about his team.

"So based on that premise, which hand on the stick man do you think can help them find that love for one another again?" asked Joe.

Grasping the concept much better now, Coach answered confidently, "Neither."

"You sure?" asked Joe, giving him one more chance to think more deeply about his answer. "Listen closely to my question, Coach. Which hand can *help* them find that love again?" Joe smiled knowing well he was being a bit confusing. "Please understand, Coach, there is truly a place where both hands can be beneficial to one's growth, even in the area of love."

Joe reached across his desk and picked up a picture of his two sons when they were in grade school. "When my children were young, I'd occasionally reward them for working well together on a project. This encouraged them to repeat the action. On the other hand, there were also times I'd punish them for fighting, or for not working well together, which discouraged them from repeating the action. Both tactics worked."

He looked at the picture he was holding in his hands. Shaking his head in disbelief, he interrupted his own thought. "Time goes by fast . . . Seems like just yesterday I was out in the yard playing ball with these two little guys. Now one's startin' his own business, and the other's a lawyer. Boy, what I'd give to go back for just a day."

As if coming out of a daze, Joe looked back up at Coach. "Sorry . . . lost my train of thought. Now, what was I saying? Oh yeah, punishing and rewarding my kids worked in the short run, and was the right thing to do. But over time, I had to make sure they began to see for themselves the benefits of making the *choice* to work together on their own. And not just the external benefits, but the internal ones, like peace and joy, which are much more meaningful in the long run. The peace and joy they experienced as a result of their *choosing* to work together, and in essence love each other, over time became far more a motivating factor than either the rewards or the punishments."

Coach stood up as if he was really starting to see the light now and walked over to the whiteboard. "So although you used both hands to help them along, that wasn't what really pushed them over the top. What really pushed them was when they themselves began to see the deeper benefits that come from loving one another."

"Exactly!" exclaimed Joe, more excited now than Coach had ever seen him. "The key thing to remember here is *deeper benefits,* 'cause we'll come back to that in a few minutes."

"Okay," Joe continued, "let's take the last one, but certainly not the least: *passion*. If you want to help your players find the passion for the game again, which hand will you use?"

"Well, a little of both, I guess. Passion is a tough thing to force on someone. But there are times when a foot in the rear can inspire a burst of passion pretty nicely." A guilty smile came across Coach's face.

Joe nodded in agreement and reiterated, "A burst, right?"

"Yeah . . . a short-term fix," Coach said reassuringly. "And, on the other hand, although you can't really 'buy' someone's passion over the long haul . . ."

"Stop right there," interrupted Joe, leaning back in his chair and crossing his arms. "Why not? I mean, I think I could be pretty passionate if you paid me a million dollars to mop the gym floor every day."

"Maybe, Joe, but over time, after I pay you the million, you'll go right back to your old ways . . . until I offer you two million, that is."

"Perfect! You hit the nail on the head. It'll never be enough, will it? I'll always want more. There's a term for that. It's called *greed*, something our society is noted for," Joe said. "So what's so dangerous about that on a team?"

"Greed breeds selfishness. People become more concerned about what they can *get* for themselves than about what they can *give* to their teammates, a dangerous combination. And one I've become all too familiar with this season," said Coach, feeling good about the progress of the conversation.

"Right. So now finish your original thought: 'Although you can't really buy someone's passion over the long haul . . .'"

"I was just saying that the 'treasure,' or in my case, winning, can inspire short bursts of passion, but over the course of time, you need much more than that to drive passion." Coach stopped as if stuck on the last point he'd made. "Guess I'm still not 100 percent sure I know what would drive passion over the long-term, Joe. I mean, with my team the guys have all lost it. And although I've used both the treasure and the hatchet to inspire short bursts of passion, I don't really see it in any of them right now. I guess you just have it or you don't?"

For the first time in the last half hour, Coach felt dejected again. "I guess if you really think about it, passion, love, and will are all pretty similar in that respect. They're things that come from within—you can't really force them onto anyone. They have to want it themselves, from the inside out."

Coach dropped his head as if he'd just realized his efforts were hopeless. He'd come all this way only to find out that he couldn't fix it. He was stuck with a bunch of selfish kids who had no will to win, no love for their teammates, and definitely no passion for the game. What was worse, he was convinced, having already worn out both hands of the stick man, there was nothing else he could do to change it. It was now up to the players: they had to choose to change.

Joe stood up and walked over to the board and briefly studied the illustration. "Coach, I want you to look closely at this

Will
Love
Passion

stick man, because he represents the majority of leaders in our culture today. CEOs like your friend Grant, vice presidents, restaurant managers, even pastors, teachers, and parents—in fact, Coach, he's a pretty accurate depiction of you, too. Yep, unfortunately, I think you'll find that most leaders fall into this category at some point in their lives, because most leaders have been and may continue to be heavily motivated by both of these hands. And—" Joe almost whispered—"*what most moves us to action usually determines how we attempt to move others to action.*"

Joe paused briefly before continuing. "You see, God wired us all to be motivated by rewards and fear, but in a healthy way. Not in the way our self-seeking culture has twisted it. Desiring a reward for something is not wrong in and of itself. In fact, all you have to do is go back to the story of David and Goliath in the Bible to see that. David, upon walking on the scene, almost immediately asked, 'What will be given to the man that slays the Philistine giant?' He desired a reward for sticking his neck out. But he also desired to follow God's direction in his life and had a deep faith in God, trusting him to secure the victory over Goliath. He was a man after God's heart. He was dearly loved and used in a mighty way by God. So his desire for a reward for slaying the giant was not rebuked or looked down upon in any way by God.

"God expects us to have a reverent fear of him, too . . . like the healthy and respectful fear a child might have of his or her own father. The book of Proverbs tells us that 'The fear of the Lord is the beginning of wisdom.' And countless other verses encourage us in this area. It's pretty clear that the fear thing is a key part of how we're wired to behave." Joe looked at Coach to make sure he was staying with him before continuing on.

"The problem in our society occurs when either of these two things becomes more than what they were originally supposed to be. Like when we allow ourselves to be driven by the treasure so much that we become completely self-absorbed—the more we get, the more we want. Then as we get more, our entire identity begins to revolve around how much we have. In many cases, it becomes an addiction to pursue even more. After all, it eventually defines us; it's who we become. So over time, we lose sight of the bigger picture, the one that includes who we were really designed to be. Unfortunately, our families and friends usually bear the brunt of these misguided desires. Remember: treasure can be a lot of things. Like with you, it's probably winning . . . and also control, status, or a number of other related motivators. That's your treasure. With others, it's titles, money, power, sex, or all sorts of things." Joe stood for a moment in silence to allow the thought to sink in.

"Of course, the fear of losing those things can serve as our hatchet as we go through life, too. And the real sad part of it is, when we're put into a position to influence others, instead of influencing them as we *should,* we lead them from the perspective of our own pursuits. We become willing to offer great rewards to those who will help us pursue our desires and harsh punishments to anyone who dares stand in the way of those desires. And you know what? Most of the time, it works . . . for a season, anyway.

"Wall Street is full of companies that rely heavily on the hatchet and the treasure, and are very successful, I might add. But at some point, there has to be more, because eventually the treasure will lose its luster. When the desire for more outruns the supply, that's when things get real dicey for leaders. You see, as long as there's plenty of treasure to throw out there, people will put up with all sorts of hatchets. But stop giving them more treasure—more money, more wins, more control, or whatever—and the hatchet will lose its edge, too."

It was evident by the look on Coach's face that he was getting it and was now beginning to reflect upon the season. "Okay, Joe," said Coach, wanting to get back to the discussion of his team. "I agree that most of us, as leaders, probably have an unhealthy view toward the hatchet and the treasure, which leads us to pursue our treasure in an unhealthy and selfish manner. And I can see how leaders . . . how *I* . . . have in turn overused those motivators with my team in hopes of getting them back on the winning track. Really, in pursuit of my own desires. But I gotta ask: What other options are there? I mean, if it's my fault they've lost their will, love, and passion, it seems like it ought to be my responsibility to help them get it back, right?"

"Well, you're partially right. Something like that is never *completely* any one person's fault, even a leader's," answered Joe, "because each individual still has their own choices to make in terms of their attitudes, desires, and actions in response to those they're supposed to be following. But be that as it may, you're still primarily responsible for their loss of those things, because, to a large extent, as their leader you've led them down the wrong path." Joe stopped and looked at Coach, waiting for him to acknowledge the truth in his statement. Coach gave him an affirming nod. "So, in effect, you should feel responsible to lead them back."

Coach looked up at Joe almost desperately. "But how? Lord knows I've already used up both hands on the stick man. What's left?"

Joe picked up a red marker and walked over to the whiteboard. Turning to Coach, he began again. "Look at this picture again. What's missing? I mean the hands and feet are there, the head's there, but there's still one thing missing from this picture that pulls everything together. Do you see it?" Joe asked excitedly as Coach stared at the picture with a blank look on his face.

"Let me ask you another way: What is it that connects the head and the hands, that brings real life to the person?"

"The *heart!*" Coach exclaimed. "*The heart!*" Joe reached across the center of the stick man and drew a big heart.

"Exactly. This guy is simply going through the motions until you add a heart. But once you add the heart, *bam!* he comes to life. Because the heart is the lifeblood from which everything flows. It's not only our internal pump and filter, it's also the conduit that allows us to connect with others. So, if you want to truly lead others effectively, you must start by leading from your heart." Joe put the cap back on the marker he was using and made his way back to his chair.

"Okay," said Coach. "This is great, and makes a lot of sense, especially in athletics, but now what?"

"Well, now comes the tough part."

Will
Love
Passion

"What?" asked Coach, astonished.

"You heard me. Now's the tough part. Because leading with the heart is not all it's cracked up to be. In fact, I might as well warn you right now, it's much, much more difficult than simply leading with the hatchet or the treasure."

"But I thought we agreed that the hatchet and the treasure don't work?" asked Coach, sounding more confused now.

"No, they don't work the *best* over the long haul," said Joe, correcting Coach. "Remember, they both work very well in the short run, but if you're looking for *lasting* effect, they just don't cut it—without the heart, that is. It's only when they're all working together in proper proportion that things really begin to click. And that's very hard to achieve," said Joe. "Fact is, very few leaders ever get it right. And even the ones that do, struggle. They may try, or they may in some cases look like they're trying, but when it comes down to it, most miss the true essence of what leading with the heart is really all about."

Joe opened a drawer to his desk and pulled out a yellow notepad. "Coach, I really have enjoyed our time this morning, but I have a 6:30 appointment that should be here any minute."

No sooner than Joe finished his sentence a knock came at the door. "Good morning, Sarah. Just one minute, please."

"No problem," came a voice from outside the door.

"Joe . . . you have to help me on this. I feel like I'm starting to get it now, but I still have a lot of questions. When can we meet again?" Joe glanced at his computer screen.

"Let's see. I assume morning is best for you since I think you're fairly busy after school these days," Joe said, a smirk on his face, "but mornings are pretty full for me until . . . until Friday. How does Friday morning, 5:15, sound?"

"Great," said Coach. "I'll be here. Thanks, Joe. You know, I really enjoyed this time, too." Coach grabbed his stuff and politely greeted Sarah as he headed through the doorway toward his office to start the day.

As he walked down the hall, his head was spinning. *What the heck just happened in there?* he wondered. *What is it about Joe that makes him so darn . . .* Coach couldn't think of a term to accurately describe him. He was kind, smart, creative, compassionate . . . He was like no other person he'd ever met before. And yet, he was a janitor. *This guy should be teaching philosophy at some college,* Coach thought to himself as he made his way back to his office.

Chapter 10

The Real Reason

The bell rang, signaling the end of third hour, and as usual, the students in Coach Rocker's biology class shot up and headed out the door as quickly as possible, trying to keep the day moving. Coach, in his normal routine between classes, turned to face his computer and check his e-mail before the next group of students found their way into his classroom. But before he could open his first one, a voice interrupted him.

"Mr. Rocker, can I ask you a question?" It was Sarah Keller, the young lady who was meeting with Joe when Coach was leaving earlier that morning.

"Sure, Sarah. What's up?" Coach said, hoping to speed the conversation along.

"Why do you teach?" asked Sarah in her normal, shy tone.

"I . . . I guess 'cause I like to. I mean, I like to . . . you know, help you kids learn." *Whew,* Coach thought. *I got out of that one . . . barely.* He knew that the real reason he taught was because he had to in order to land a coaching job. But he also knew it would speak poorly of his motives if he let on to that. "Why do you ask, Sarah?"

"Well . . . I've been working a lot with Mr. Taylor lately on that question, so I decided I would do some research of my own. You know, ask my teachers the same question, then compare their responses with what I see from them as teachers."

Coach's heart sank into his stomach. He knew he was probably one of the worst teachers in the high school, but he also knew that his coaching skills had always gotten him his jobs in the first place. Teaching was what he had to do to make a living. Coaching . . . now *that* was his passion.

Sarah politely thanked Coach and headed out the door. *Why do I teach? Hmmm . . . good question. Wish I didn't have to most of the time.* Shaking his head, Coach turned back to his computer screen to check his e-mail.

For the next four practices, Coach tried everything he could think of to lead from the heart. He encouraged the guys more, tried not to yell at them as much, and even cracked a smile a few times, which was typically unheard of when he was on the basketball court. But despite all his efforts, the team still seemed to be going through the motions with no real change evident.

Coach did get a few strange looks from his seniors when he stopped play to compliment one of them for screening and hustling after the ball. But still, the will to win, the love for their teammates, and the passion to play all seemed a distant memory to Coach as he watched his team painfully struggle through drills day in and day out.

Making the lonely walk to his car after Thursday's practice, Coach was feeling pretty down as he considered his team's response to his attempts at leading from the heart. *What is wrong with them?* he wondered. *Why do they still seem to be missing it? Maybe all this heart stuff was a bunch of crap after all.* As he turned the key in the ignition of his car, his cell phone buzzed. He flipped it open.

"Coach, how the heck are ya?" came a voice from what seemed like a party on the other end of the line.

"Grant? I'm . . . I'm all right, I guess. How are you?" answered Coach, barely able to hear anything but all the background noise.

"I'm great! Listen, I just popped into Paul's Pub and wondered if you wanted to join me for a quick drink on your way home?"

"You know what? That sounds great. Kathy and the kids always spend Thursday evenings at her parents', so I'm batchin' it tonight anyway. Be there in fifteen."

"Great! See you then," said Grant before clicking the phone off.

About fifteen minutes later, Coach walked through the front entrance of the bustling little pub just down the street from Grant's office. Doing a quick scan of the room, he found Grant at his usual place, surrounded by all the up-and-comers in the local business community.

Everyone knew Grant, knew what he did, and always seemed to be drawn to his success. In addition, the news of his separation from his wife had gotten out so that now, even more than in past weeks, the group included an unusually high number of attractive young women.

"My favorite coach in the world!" Grant yelled when he caught a glimpse of Coach walking across the room. It was obvious he'd been there for a while already. "First one's on me," Grant said, signaling to the bartender to get whatever Coach wanted. "So how are the guys lookin' for tomorrow night's big match-up?" Grant asked as Coach grabbed a seat next to him at the bar.

"Great question. Who knows? I tried some different tactics this week at practice and am still not getting a good feel for things as far as a change of heart goes. The guys just keep going through the motions, like they *have* to be there instead of *wanting* to be there. Who knows?" Coach threw his hands up in the air in a surrendering gesture and shook his head.

"New tactics?" asked Grant. "Whaddya mean? You got the guys doin' yoga now?" They both laughed at the picture that thought created in their minds.

"No, I just had a really interesting conversation with Joe again on Monday, and it made a lot of sense. But as I tried to implement some of the ideas, nothing changed. I'm beginning to think it's just this group of guys. I just have a bad group of kids right now. I don't think anything will work with 'em." Coach took a drink, then set his glass back down on the bar.

"So what'd ya change?" asked Grant.

"I changed the hatchet-treasure concept . . ."

"You what?" Grant practically yelled while he gave Coach a look of astonishment.

"I changed the hatchet-treasure concept thing. Added something to it."

"Coach, Coach, Coach, what are you thinking? You know how long I've been doing what I do?" Grant was obviously in his element and feeling pretty good about himself. "You know how much success I've had over the years? You see all these people, especially these nice young ladies standing around me?" His voice lowered a bit as he motioned for Coach to look around. "I didn't get to the top by being wishy-washy, if ya know what I mean. Coach, you gotta stick with it. You gotta stay after 'em. They'll wake up—you just gotta keep doing what you do. Come on, buddy. You're the most successful coach in Kentucky. Why would you want to change now?" Grant finally stopped to catch his breath and take a sip of his drink.

"I didn't scrap the whole thing. I just learned a new way

to look at it. And it made a lot of sense. In fact, you know all the questions we've been talking about lately?" Grant nodded. "Well, I can't completely put my finger on *how* yet, but I have a feeling this new approach will answer them. Or at least I did earlier this week." Coach looked back down at his drink now, remembering how his players failed to respond to his changes.

One of Grant's friends walked up and interrupted the conversation, so Coach sat alone with his thoughts for a moment. Maybe Grant was right . . . maybe he did need to stick to his original plan. After all, Grant obviously knew what he was talking about. He'd been through it all on his climb to the top. All you had to do was *look* at him and you could see. He was truly a picture of success. All eyes seemed to be on Grant, and he loved it. In fact, he seemed like the happiest guy in the world right now, even with the family struggles he was dealing with.

Coach interrupted Grant's conversation, well aware that this was the only way he was going to get a word in edgewise. "Okay, Grant, so what happened to all the questions you were struggling with a few weeks ago? Did you get 'em answered? I mean, you obviously seem like you're back to your old self, back to living life to the fullest again. What happened?"

Grant put his arm around his friend and leaned in to him. "Coach . . . two things. One, I decided that I needed to suck it up and make it happen like I've always done in the past. And two . . . well, it worked. Our earnings came in above expectations for the first time in three quarters. Plus, we just signed a huge contract with Intelit that'll shoot us through the next two quarters. Stock shot through the roof this week. Bonuses will be back, and everyone knows it. The mood has been incredible. The good ol' dollar has come through again. And I'm ridin' the wave, baby!" Grant crouched down and got into his best surfing pose.

"That's great; congratulations," said Coach as he raised his drink to Grant in a toast. "I still have to ask you, though. The questions . . . did they all go away? I mean, I guess now you know *why* you do what you do, since the money's back, right? People are motivated again. They want to come to work because the dollar just grew. You can use the hatchet, and people will respond big time out of fear of losing their piece of the pie. Everything's better—family, friends . . . everything?"

Grant shot a dirty look at Coach, obviously feeling the low blow he had just sarcastically thrown at him about his family. "Hey, that's life. There are some things you just can't control. I can't control Cindy, and you know that. I can only control what *I* control. If I dwell on the things I can't control, they'll eat me alive. Plus, I'll be ineffective as a leader. I have to stay focused and on top of the things I *can* control."

"Hey, I understand," replied Coach. "I guess I'm wrestling with the fact that I think my *treasure*, winning, has become an obsession with me, and I've spent the last ten years of my life pursuing it over everything else—and imposing that obsession on those I've had the most influence on, too. And I wonder . . . I guess I just wonder if that's right. On top of that, Joe helped me discover that there are a number of things that neither the treasure nor the hatchet will motivate."

Grant took another drink, set his glass on the bar, and looked Coach straight in the eyes. "Listen, don't get me wrong, I'm sure there's validity to what your janitor buddy's been tellin' ya; but remember, we're still livin' in the real world. People come to work for a paycheck. They have to in order to put food on the table. And your guys play ball to win. It's that simple. That's why you and I do what *we* do, too. We're just a little more driven than the next guy, and that's why we're at the top of the food chain. So I'm not sure what things the hatchet or the treasure won't work on, but I do know what they *will* work on. And *that's* what good leaders focus on."

Coach finished his drink and stood up; the conversation was going nowhere. "I should get home . . . big game tomorrow night, ya know. I need to make sure we're ready." Coach put his jacket on. "I hope things keep going well for you, Grant. Keep ridin' the wave."

"Thanks, buddy! Hope they get better for you soon, too. And good luck tomorrow night." Grant patted Coach on the back as he headed out through the crowd of people.

When he got home, Coach walked through the front door and into a dark house. Kathy and the kids were still at her mom's, so after flipping some lights on, he headed straight for the kitchen to find something quick to eat. As he sat, his mind went back to the bar—and Grant. *What a dream life . . . Grant really has the best of everything. Or does he? Three weeks ago he was struggling with every aspect of life imaginable. Now, after just one week of financial success, he's back on cloud nine. Is it real? Will it last?* Coach couldn't help wondering to himself. *Is he really as happy as he seemed, or is he just riding a superficial high—from the boost in the stock, the people at the bar, the alcohol? Who knows?* Life appeared to be back on track for Grant, but it certainly wasn't for Coach, and he knew it. He could hardly wait to meet with Joe the next morning to try to get to the real heart of the matter.

Chapter 11

Listening to Hear

Wanting to make sure he wasn't rushed with Joe, Coach showed up ten minutes early the next morning. When he peeked through the door, he saw Joe with his head in his hands and his eyes closed, apparently sleeping. As much as Coach hated interrupting his sleep, he was anxious to get started, so he cleared his throat, hoping to signal to Joe that he was standing there.

Joe opened his eyes and looked up at Coach. "Good morning, my friend!"

"Good morning . . . Sorry to wake you."

"Oh, I wasn't sleeping. I was listening . . . to a friend, that is."

Doing a double-take of the room, Coach checked to see if he'd somehow missed someone else standing there with them. "Uh . . . mind me asking who you were listening to?"

"Not at all. I was listening to God."

"Okaaay," Coach said, a look of bewilderment on his face. Joe smiled at his friend reassuringly.

"It's okay, Coach. Most other people don't get it either. They think you're only supposed to *talk* to God. You know, '*pray* without ceasing' somehow gets interpreted as '*talk* without ceasing.' Unfortunately, to most that means always telling God what they want. You know, kinda like he's this giant genie in a bottle waiting to grant our every wish. Truth is, what he

97

really wants is for us to know him—to *truly* know him. 'Cause when we truly get to know him, we begin to understand his love for us and how that plays out in all our relationships. And how well do you suppose you'll ever get to know someone if all you ever do is talk to them and tell them what you want?"

"Probably not very well," Coach answered, feeling a bit convicted now at how he himself had always viewed prayer.

"Don't get me wrong, Coach, God wants us to bring our requests to him in prayer." Joe walked over to a small refrigerator located under the coffee pot and opened it. "He loves us more than we love our own kids, so naturally he wants us to come to him when we're hurting or in need. But he also longs to just *be* with us, too. You know . . . to be in quiet communion with us. Like a gentle breeze on a hot summer afternoon. He wants us to take the time to just feel his presence. And yet, in our hurried culture, it's next to impossible to get quiet. With cell phones, iPods, laptops, and e-mails, we're constantly connected with everyone but God himself." As he finished his thought, Joe walked over to the coffee pot and poured Coach a cup of coffee.

Coach hadn't planned on the conversation going anywhere near religion, but since they were on the topic, he couldn't resist trying to get a few of his own burning questions answered. "Okay, since we're on the subject, how does religion play into the whole hatchet-heart-treasure thing we've been talking about? To be honest, my experiences with religion tell me that the hatchet and the treasure are really all there is. To me, it seems that everything at church revolves around a set of rules and rituals. And if we don't adhere, there's hell to pay—literally," sighed Coach.

"Does sound a little like a hatchet mentality," said Joe.

"A little?" Coach shot back. "The church I grew up in was all about rules and rituals. You know, going through the motions. If you broke any of the rules, or stopped following the rituals, look out! God was just waiting to whack you upside your head. By the time I got to college, I was fed up. I couldn't do it anymore, so I quit going to church altogether.

"Of course, watching my older brother go to the other extreme didn't help my opinion of the church, either. He did everything you could possibly imagine to try to earn the 'favor of God,' as his pastor always called it. Reality was, he was just trying to work his way into heaven. In the end, it pretty much destroyed his life." Coach dropped his head, upset by the thought of his brother.

"Lost his wife and kids, and most of his old friends, too. Pretty ugly stuff. Either way, all I see in the church is a bunch of hypocrites. They go to church and do their thing on Sunday, and then Monday through Friday they live completely different. It makes no sense to me." Joe listened intently, as he could tell his friend was deeply bitter toward the church.

After a few moments of silence, Joe posed a few questions to Coach. "You know, Coach, religion . . . the whole faith thing . . . really does provide the perfect illustration for the hatchet-heart-treasure concept in action, at its worst and at its best.

"You see, the first picture you painted was of a religious focus centered on rules and rituals, going through the motions out of fear of punishment. You know, step out of line, and *whack!* God's standing up there with a hatchet in his hand ready to take a big swing at you. And since everything you were taught appeared to revolve around those things, that became your picture of God, right?"

"Yep. That pretty much sums it up," answered Coach.

"So what happened?" asked Joe as he sipped his coffee.

"I eventually got frustrated. Actually, I guess I even got angry . . . and maybe became bitter about the whole church thing."

"Right. So the hatchet, when perceived as the central theme of everything, really drove you *away* from God rather than *to* him, right?"

"Yeah . . . I guess that's right," agreed Coach, nodding. "I didn't really want anything to do with it since all it caused me was pain and guilt."

"Okay, now go the other way. Think about your brother. All he did was work, work, work. His central focus was on trying to earn rewards—'blessings,' as he defined them. That was his main motive. He tried to do as much good as he could. But in the end, he found it was never really enough. Life was still hard, full of the normal ups and downs we all go through. All the accolades and praise he received from his pastor, or even his friends, were never enough. So he just kept reaching for more and more and more, trying to earn his way to heaven—at the expense of everyone else in his life. Remember, when we get caught up in seeking treasures ahead of everything else, what happens?"

Coach thought for a second. "You begin to focus on yourself more than others. You become greedy. But I'm not sure I understand how greed is related to what my brother was pursuing in the church."

Joe removed his reading glasses and leaned forward. "Coach, anything—let me say it again, *anything*—we pursue that causes a deterioration in the relationships God designed for us, like the relationship with him, or the relationship within our commitment of marriage, is a selfish, unhealthy, and, yes, greedy pursuit, even if that pursuit comes from within the church building."

"It's always pained me to watch people pursue a ministry 'in the name of God' while simultaneously neglecting their relationship with God and with their family and friends. It never—I repeat, *never*—works, especially in the long run!"

"That's exactly what happened to my brother," said Coach. "He was so focused on trying to earn God's blessings through what he *did* that he failed to nurture God's love in his relationships."

"Right," replied Joe, "like his relationship with God, followed by his relationship with his family. He's bitter toward church now because he feels like *it* caused the breakdown," Joe said, more as a statement than a question.

"Ohhh yeah," said Coach. "That's an understatement. You can't even mention God or the church around him without getting a fifteen-minute lecture on how screwed up the whole religion thing really is."

Joe shook his head in disappointment. "That's really sad, Coach. I mean, it's just not the picture Jesus painted for us at all. And yet, it seems like there are millions of people today who've left the church or their 'religion' for these same reasons. The hatchet or the treasure was wrongly emphasized as the central focus of God's plan. It's just not what Jesus modeled when he walked this earth.

"In essence, the pursuit of good works and 'blessings' was your brother's treasure. And because that was his central focus, things eventually fell apart. For you, you were focused on all the rules: fear was your central focus. And that's why things fell apart for you, too."

Joe turned to Coach. "Please understand, doing good works

is a key element of our faith in action. And having a respectful fear of God, like we talked about Monday, is a critical component of our faith, too. After all, he *is* God and *does* have the capability to do whatever he determines to be best for us, even when that includes bestowing 'blessings' we may not at first like or see as blessings. God desires for us to embrace both a healthy fear and a healthy desire for rewards as part of our faith."

Joe stood up now and walked over to the whiteboard to clarify his point. "But when either of them becomes the central driving force of our faith—in other words, when they become more of a factor in our lives than our personal relationship with God or our relationships with others—we eventually end up frustrated, angry, and even bitter."

Joe picked up the red marker again and traced over the heart in the middle of the stick drawing. "But when the heart is truly the central focus of our faith, the main drive behind our actions, we experience the true joy, peace, and contentment that Jesus desired for us to experience in this life. And, although we're still moved to action by both—a fear of God and a desire for eternal rewards—it's the relationship aspect that trumps everything. That's the central focus of the heart as God designed it to be."

It was obvious by the tone of Joe's voice that he was passionate about this topic. "Think about it. That's why Jesus was constantly on the religious and political leaders of his day: they were all about the hatchet and the treasure. They knew biblical law like the back of their hands, but they judged people harshly, attempting to shame them into compliance with their rules and their rituals. They also promoted the pursuit of works and deeds as the means to enter God's kingdom. On top of that, they used, or should I say *mis*used, their religious and political clout to wrongly obtain personal wealth." Joe shook his head in frustration as he pointed at both the hatchet and the treasure in the stick man's hands.

"Jesus came on the scene and basically blew both of those concepts, as central themes, out of the water. Instead, his teachings centered on *love:* love for God and for others. In other words, relationships. That's what he taught, that's how he led his disciples, and that's the example he showed when he interacted with others, too. His influence was always centered on relationships first. 'Faith, hope, and love . . . and the greatest of these is *love!*'"

Joe stood quietly for a moment as he looked at the drawing. "Coach, if you really stop and think about it, this model still works in leadership today. Go back to the things we talked about earlier in the week that your guys have lost: the will to win, the love for their teammates, and the passion for the game. These things are key elements of success with any team, right? And they *all* come from the heart."

Joe again pointed to the words on the board. "You can't force someone to love their

Will
Love
Passion

teammates, nor can you buy their love . . . or their will or passion, for that matter. Nope; those things have to come from within—from the heart." He drew three arrows connecting the three words with the heart, then put the marker down and walked back over to his seat.

Chapter 12

First Things First

Coach jumped up and walked toward the board to take his own turn at the drawing. "Okay. This is great. It makes sense . . . these things definitely come from the heart. But I still don't really understand what my role is, as a leader, in helping my kids find these things. I tried to lead with the heart all week, and it didn't change a d— thing!" He tapped his finger repeatedly on the stick man's heart, emphasizing his point. "I mean, I encouraged 'em, I was more patient with 'em. I even smiled at 'em, and nothing! Let's be honest. I don't control their hearts. I can motivate them with the hatchet and the treasure, but I can't change their hearts. They have to want it, and right now, they don't want it and there's nothing I can do to them that'll change that." Deeply discouraged by the thought, he turned and walked back to his chair.

Again Joe leaned forward, preparing to make another important point. "Coach, you're right. You can't change their hearts. There really is nothing you can do *to* them that will change that. But there is one thing you can do, as a leader, that will impact their hearts more powerfully than any hatchet or treasure could even come close to." Coach leaned forward, mirroring Joe's posture, as he listened intently. Almost in a whisper, Joe continued. "Coach . . . you can change your own heart *first*. That's the best way to deeply affect the hearts of those you lead: *Change your own heart first.*"

Coach sat back in his chair, looked at the ceiling, and sighed. He looked back at Joe in frustration. "But what is it I need to change? I mean, I feel like I've changed *everything* this year. Think about the adjustments I made with both the hatchet and the treasure. I turned them both up and down like a stovetop burner. Nothing worked, but they were changes. Then, once I finally figured this heart thing out, I adjusted my methods and began to lead with the heart. You know, with more encouragement and less yelling, more smiling—still nothing worked."

Joe listened with empathy in his eyes as Coach finished venting. "I understand, Coach. You really have worked hard and made all the adjustments one could possibly imagine in a season. But the adjustments you've made have all had to do with the *what* and the *how* of leading. In other words, you made adjustments to *what* you were doing in practice, like running more sprints, or working more on defense, or adjusting your offense. You also made adjustments to *how* you were doing what you were doing, like being more encouraging or more patient, or smiling more. And those are all important aspects of coaching. However, they are still not the most important aspect of coaching—or *leading,* for that matter . . . not by a long shot. Coach, the thing that truly separates the good leaders from the great ones starts with a simple, three-letter word: *why.*"

Joe walked back up to the board and off to the side wrote the word WHY in big, bold letters. "That's right, recognizing the power behind the question why is what I call the 'X-factor' in leadership. But remember now, I said it was just the start. There's more to it than simply answering the question. And this is where the change of heart comes into play."

Joe walked back over to his desk and picked up a small model jet he had sitting off to the side. "Coach, imagine this were a real jet. *Why* does it exist? I mean, what's its purpose?"

"To get people from point A to point B," said Coach.

"Okay," said Joe. "Suppose you wanted to visit some relatives in Seattle, and you got on this jet in Chicago and flew to Seattle. Once you got there, the plane turned around immediately and flew you back to Chicago. Did it serve its purpose?"

Coach thought for a moment. "Yeah . . . well, no . . . I mean, I wanted to go to Seattle to see relatives, and if it immediately turned around and flew me back to Chicago, I didn't get to see my relatives, so I guess it didn't serve its purpose."

"Wait a minute. You said it existed to get you from point A to point B. It did that, right?" Joe asked.

"Yeah . . . it did," said Coach.

"So, then, it served its purpose," said Joe.

"Well, kinda . . . I guess it did what it was supposed to do. But since I didn't get to see my relatives, it didn't help me achieve *my* purpose for getting on the plane in the first place," replied Coach.

"So, if I hear you right, when you get on that plane, you have your *own* purpose for doing so, right?" asked Joe, still holding the model in his hands. "So which one's more important—the jet's purpose or yours?"

"Mine," Coach answered, not real sure of himself.

"Well, if that's the case, have fun walking, because the plane can't land you at your relatives' home. Remember, you said its purpose was to get you from point A to point B, Chicago to Seattle in this case."

"Okay . . . I guess the plane's purpose is more important?" Coach came back now with just a little more confidence.

"Not exactly," Joe replied, chuckling at his friend's confusion. "Remember, if the jet lands in Seattle and then immediately heads back to Chicago, with no consideration for your purpose, its purpose really doesn't matter much in the end, does it? Imagine a jet created to fly back and forth from point A to point B empty—pretty worthless, huh?" Joe paused to let the question sink in a bit.

"Coach, you seem like you're a guy determined to be the best that you can be in this life. Am I right?" asked Joe.

"Absolutely!" Coach exclaimed. "I get up every morning with that thought rolling around in my head."

"That's what I would expect to hear from you," said Joe. "But you see, when we ask ourselves the question *why* we do what we do, if the answer doesn't take into consideration first why we were actually created, we're destined to fall short of fulfilling the actual reason for our existence. In doing so, we fail to be the *best* that we were designed to be." Joe looked down at the model in sadness, then looked back at Coach. "This jet can fly back and forth from Seattle to Chicago a million times, and on its millionth trip it can even have a big celebration for so many successful flights. But if it doesn't fulfill the *real* reason for its existence—to help people fulfill *their* purpose by transporting them safely to their destinations—it really isn't serving its primary purpose at all. Therefore, it's falling short of being the best that it can be.

"Make no mistake, Coach—the jet can fly back and forth from Seattle to Chicago empty much faster and more efficiently without the hassle of all those pesky passengers. But then again, what would it really be accomplishing in the end?" Joe set the model back down on his desk.

It was easy to see by the look on Coach's face that the

analogy hit home with him. As he reflected upon his own life, he could see how he had been going after his pursuits much like an empty jet, failing to seriously consider the passengers along the way. In effect, the rush of attention, power, and success he felt from winning, followed closely by his fear of failure, had become the central focus of his pursuits, becoming the real reason why he did what he did.

After a brief pause to refill the coffees, Joe continued. "We may succeed in our goals in life; we may become the winningest coach in the state, or climb to the top of the corporate ladder, or gain the respect of our dads, or friends, or millions of others. We may gain wealth or power beyond belief, or even pastor a church of ten thousand people. But if in our heart of hearts our *why* is more focused on those things—and the rush that comes with them—than on our true purpose, we're not living up to our potential. In essence, we're not really being the *best* we can be because we're not living up to who we were created to be. It may not look like it from the outside, and sometimes, it may not even feel like it. But when something fails to serve its ultimate purpose, its *reason* for existence, the reality is, it's failing—period!

"Remember what I said earlier? Jesus taught over and over that our very existence was all about relationships—first with him, and then with others. That's why God created us in the first place. So it stands to reason that when your *why* answer is self-centered, your purpose, your very reason for existence, is not being fulfilled. And in the long run, you'll not experience the true peace and joy this life has to offer."

Joe leaned back in his chair and clasped his hands behind his head. "Remember a few weeks ago when you and I were talking about leadership and selfishness, and I told you that selfishness was the great differentiator between good leaders and great leaders?"

"Yeah . . . I remember. I never really did fully understand what that meant, but I remember," said Coach.

"And do you remember me from time to time talking about there being a *reason* for everything?"

Coach cracked a half smile as he shot back at Joe, "Oh yeah. I remember those comments all too well. Lost a lot of sleep trying to figure them out, you know."

"Well," said Joe, a sly grin on his face, "that's what we're talking about here. When you consider the *reason* you do what you do as a coach, you're asking yourself the *why* question. If you really want to get it right, you must remember that you were created for relationships; therefore, you have to consider your guys first. In fact, you have to consider all the relationships in your life. And when you do that, your answer to the question *why* becomes much bigger than just you. The best leaders' legacies produce what Jesus called 'good fruit,' lived out through others way after they themselves have gone by the wayside. But everything starts with selfless thinking. Will I lead for my reasons or for the benefit of others? Remember, making the *choice* to lead for the benefit of others means your leading from the heart, with love. Prioritizing relationships."

"You know, I never really thought of leadership that way," said Coach with growing enthusiasm in his voice. "But it does make sense. When the answer to the *why* question is more about others than about yourself, it makes a big difference in everything you do. Think about some of the greatest leaders in history: Abraham Lincoln, Mother Teresa, Martin Luther King Jr. If you would've asked any of them why they did what they did, they would've been able to answer you in a heartbeat:

they all knew their purpose in life. And in each case, it clearly centered on others much more than on themselves."

"Right!" exclaimed Joe. "They were all passionately focused on the interests of others, not on themselves. Interestingly, in each of their cases, there was a central focus on a relationship with their Creator, too."

"And like you said, Joe, their legacies lived on, producing 'good fruit' even after they were gone," added Coach.

"Yep," said Joe. "Now contrast that with people like Adolf Hitler or Joseph Stalin, who were clearly focused on their own agendas and their own pursuits of treasure—power and superiority. Big difference, right? Not only in the destruction they accomplished during their reign, but the physical, mental, and emotional pain they caused millions and millions of people that lived on for decades after they were gone."

"Wow . . . Pretty powerful stuff, when you really stop and think about it," said Coach.

"Yes, it is," replied Joe. "Unfortunately, in our culture today, with the allure of fortune, fame, and power running rampant, due in large part to the explosion of what the modern media pounds into our heads day in and day out, it's pretty easy for a leader to fall into the same category as Hitler or Stalin . . . in terms of the level of self-centered focus, that is." Joe paused to let the magnitude of his thought sink in a bit. "They may not be willing to carry out plans that would literally destroy millions of people, but they're definitely willng to sacrifice important relationships to accomplish their own desires. All you have to do is look around you, even in your own neighborhood, to find friends or relatives who have left a path of destroyed relationships behind their own pursuits of success."

Coach jumped up and walked over to the board. "Okay, let

me see if I'm clear on where we are with all this stuff, because my head's starting to spin a bit." He grabbed a marker to help him point to the ideas as he walked through them. "The hatchet and the treasure, as motivators, are a natural part of all of our lives. However, if they become the focal point of our pursuits—in other words, the reason *why* we do what we do—we're destined to fail in being who we were really created to be and in doing what we were really designed to do. What's worse, when we think this way, we tend to lead others down the same destructive path. It's just like the example you gave of Brandon cleaning his room, regardless of which method I use to motivate. If I use either one exclusively, selfishness, bitterness, anger, or resentment will follow. But when the heart is right and I'm motivating or being motivated out of a genuine love and concern for others . . . all that changes."

Coach traced the heart on the middle of the stick man. "The heart's the lifeblood, lying at the center of everything we were created to be. The heart is also where we must look to find the answers to why we do what we do in life, our purpose for being." Coach wrote the word PURPOSE at the center of the heart and then drew a line from the heart to the WHY Joe had written earlier. "If the answer to that question is centered on selfish gains like wealth or power or even wins, or if it's centered on the fear of losing those things, then we'll ultimately be failing to live up to our true potential in life. And, in effect, as leaders, we'll fail to help others live up to their potential, too.

"But when the *heart* is right, it focuses on relationships as the priority." Coach wrote the word PEOPLE beside the heart on the board. "And it's only then that we can truly be the best we were created to be, not just for ourselves but for those we influence, too—and not just how the world defines being our best, either."

Excited by the comment Coach had just made, Joe chimed in. "Exactly! Coach, that's a great point, and I'm glad you made it. Most all of us go through life trying to be successful at something. The problem is, we pursue the success that our *culture* has defined for us rather than the success our *Maker* designed for us. Again, that's why it's so important to keep the *why* question at the forefront of our hearts and minds."

Joe stood and walked up to the board. "Right from the get-go, each of us has to come to grips with who we are in the eyes of our Creator, not just who we are in the eyes of the world. And this takes some real soul searching." Joe politely signaled for Coach to hand him the marker, then wrote the word PRAYER above the word PEOPLE on the board. "When we do this, we realize that we were created for an eternal purpose, not just a worldly purpose that ends when we breathe our last breath. If we get wrapped up in becoming the greatest engineer, or musician, or pastor, or entrepreneur, or whatever, we're really getting wrapped up in *what we do* rather than *who we are*. Make no mistake, Coach: God cares much more about who you are than about what you do!"

Joe paused for a few seconds as if considering what to say next. "Now, please understand, we're clearly called to be the very best we can be, and to maximize the gifts God has given us in *whatever* we do, regardless of what our lot in life is. The problem arises when we pursue what we *think* success is at the expense of what success really is, as defined by God. Our priorities get all out of whack." Joe wrote the word PRIORITIES under the word PEOPLE.

"Fact is, Coach, the more of the world's successes you

achieve—in other words, the more wins, or money, or control, or titles, or whatever—the more wrapped up in the pursuit you typically become," Joe said in a somber tone.

"Because pursuing these successes is really just pursuing the *treasure;* the more we get, the more we want," added Coach.

"Right. But remember, it's when it comes *at the expense of what success in our lives is supposed to mean* that it really becomes destructive," said Joe. "Success as our culture defines it can be very deceptive. It can blind you to the reality

of who you really are, or even who you've become. Eventually, if the pursuit of success really gets ahold of you, you end up living your life trying to convince others of your success. You buy more things, or you build a bigger house, or you try to associate with others you consider to be successful, all to convince those around you—and maybe yourself, too—that you've arrived. You're a real success. Until tomorrow, that is, when you wake up to fight for more." Joe handed the marker back to Coach and walked to his chair.

"So if I'm hearing you right, when we ask ourselves why we do what we do—" Coach pointed to the word PURPOSE located in the center of the heart on the board—"and our answer is unselfish and centered on the right things, like our relationship with God and with others—" now he pointed to the words PRAYER, PEOPLE, and PRIORITIES—"our purpose provides for us the basis from which to define true success. Success that lasts. Right?"

"Absolutely, Coach! You got it!" exclaimed Joe. "Everything must align with your primary purpose in life. In other words, why you do what you do should derive from why you exist in the first place and flow out from there. Once the answer to those questions is in place, you know, locked into your DNA, true success will follow. What's more, it frees you from all the trappings of the never-ending pursuit of success as the world defines it. You learn to embrace where you are instead of getting caught up in the race toward a position of prominence, or moving through life driven only by the pursuit of treasures or the fear of losing them."

Joe stood up again and walked over to the whiteboard. "May I?" He held out his hand for the marker. Joe wrote the word POSITION between the words PRAYER and PEOPLE on the board. Then he turned back to Coach.

"Let's back up just a bit. One of the most destructive myths flying around today is the myth that says you should pursue, with all your heart, whatever you're most passionate about in your life. Anything else you do is somehow . . . beneath you. This lie is simply an extension of the whole success thing we've been talking about. So many today get caught up in the notion that we're each created to fulfill one great mission in life— which, don't get me wrong, we are, in a sense. However, their picture of this great mission gets clouded by their heart's desire to achieve success as the world defines it.

"Everybody wants to build 'the great platform,' be the billionaire entrepreneur, or the mega movie star, or the president of the company. That's where their 'passion' lies. So they stumble through life with a 'Just wait until . . .' attitude, all the while failing to see the value in their current position in life today. I especially see this with young people. They pursue their 'passions' in life, the things they really enjoy doing or the things they feel most gifted doing, in many cases at the expense of how God has called them to live *today*. If God called Joseph to be a slave, Moses to live in a desert, and David to shepherd sheep, who are we to think he's called us to pursue only what we're most passionate about? Can you imagine David sitting around complaining about taking care of his father's sheep? *'This stinks. I'm a good-looking guy who has all kinds of natural leadership abilities. I'm a talented musician, a skilled warrior . . . I'm fit to be a king. Why should I shepherd these sheep? Risk my life to kill this lion? I don't think so. Just wait until I'm . . .'* Get it? Dreams are great, and passion is a powerful emotion, but both should *follow* the acceptance of our true purpose, not precede it!"

Joe wrote the word PASSION below the word PRIORITIES on the board. "When the answer to the question *why* is where it's supposed to be, you don't get caught up having to build this great 'platform' from which to perform in life. Instead, you learn to embrace the *position* God has you in today. Whether you're a student, a teacher, a factory worker, or whatever, you're called to be the best you can be in that role every day!"

Coach looked like his mind was racing at the implications of Joe's words. Joe continued, "One of my favorite authors in the Bible, Paul, wrote, 'Whatever you do, work at it with all your heart, as if working for the Lord, not for man.' Now, that doesn't say, 'Coach, as long as you're working within the boundaries of what you're most gifted in or love doing, work at it with all your heart.' No! It says, '*Whatever* you do, work at it with all your heart.' In other words, be *passionate* about it! *God's* your boss, not the school board! And remember, we can't be truly working for the Lord and simultaneously sacrificing the relationships he's put in our path. It just doesn't mesh.

Competence is never complete without connection— relationships! I think you get my

point." Joe put the marker down and walked back over to his desk as Coach studied the drawing on the whiteboard, obviously reflecting deeply on the message.

Coach glanced at the clock on the wall, which read 7:05. "Are you kidding me? We've been talking for almost two hours? I had no idea it was that late! I really need to prep a bit before my first class."

"No problem. I have some things I need to shore up before the students start coming in, too. You know, Coach, I really do enjoy our chats. It's not often anymore that I get to have this type of conversation with another adult," said Joe, winking.

"You do seem to have a steady stream of young people flowing into your office," replied Coach. "I have to ask, what's that all about?"

Joe smiled as he stood up and began gathering some of his supplies to start the day. "Oh . . . Let's just say I have a few students who want to be janitors when they grow up." Again, Joe winked as the two men went their separate ways.

About five seconds elapsed when Coach heard a yell from down the hall. "Hey, Coach! Remember: Everything starts with you . . . in *your* heart!"

Arriving back at his office, Coach took out one of his notepads and began to jot down what he remembered to be written on the whiteboard. First, he drew the stick man in the center of the page. *Okay,* he thought. *We know we're all motivated by the hatchet and the treasure to some extent. And, as a coach, I use these two methods to motivate my players, too.* He drew a hatchet in the right hand and a basketball with a W in the center in the left. *These motivators, when used exclusively, lead us to greed, selfishness, anger, and bitterness. The same things I see with the guys on my team this year,* he thought as he wrote the words *selfishness* and *greed* under the W symbol and *anger* and *bitterness* under the hatchet. *But when the heart becomes the central focus of our motivation, everything changes.* He drew a big heart in the middle of the stick man. *Everything in our lives, all of our pursuits, should be founded upon our answer to the question why—why we exist, followed by why we do what we do.* He then wrote the word *purpose* in the center of the heart. For the next twenty minutes he continued to jot notes to himself as he reflected on the conversation with Joe. He knew he needed to organize his thoughts prior to communicating these ideas to the team.

Chapter 13

Searching for the Heart

Pacing the locker room floor nervously before the game, Coach considered what he and Joe had talked about earlier that week. He knew it was time for a new approach, and Joe's methods had made sense, despite the challenge they posed to his own thinking about leadership and his purpose in life. He prepared to put into words his thoughts from the week's discussions with Joe. How could he possibly explain this? What was it that would help the guys really see the importance of this whole purpose thing? How would he get them to strive for something more than just winning? Was it too risky at this juncture of the season to switch the focus now? Maybe they were closer to turning the corner than he thought? His mind raced with conflicting thoughts.

The six-minute mark signaled the players to head into the locker room for final pregame preparations. As Coach went over the match-ups and highlighted a few key points, the players listened intently. They understood all too well the importance of the game they were about to play against their district rival, the Russelville Raiders.

"Guys, you all know this is a big game, and we need this win badly to get back in the hunt for the district championship. But tonight, I want you to shift your thinking a bit. I want you to understand that this game is about much, much more than just winning." Billy Conner instantly shot a confused look toward David Kelton, who was standing off to the side dressed in his shirt and tie. They were definitely not used to hearing words like this come out of their coach's mouth. "This game is about accomplishing something more as a team. It's about hard work and dedication, sacrifice and commitment, and persevering through even the toughest of times. And it's about doing all of this *together,* as a team. Guys, these are the things that really matter in this game. And these are the reasons you need to get out there and bust your tails like never before! Now bring it in here!" he yelled as the players quickly huddled and threw their hands together. "Let's get after it tonight, Knights. On three. One, two, three!"

"Knights!"

Unfortunately, within the first two minutes of the game, the emotion had worn off, and the Knights found themselves down 8–2 after giving up back-to-back three pointers to the Raiders' sharpshooting backcourt duo. Although the Knights fought back to tie the game up at 42 by the end of the third quarter, the Raiders had just too much firepower from outside for the visiting team. As the final buzzer sounded, the scoreboard told the story: Raiders 58, Knights 50. The Knights were now halfway through their district season, and with an overall record of 6–6, things did not look good for the rest of the year.

The players filed slowly into the locker room, dejected and spent after coming up short in another hard-fought battle. As they sat down on the benches in front of the whiteboard, Coach made his way to the front of the room.

"Guys," Coach shook his head in utter disbelief, "I really don't know what to say anymore. When we make the types of mental errors we made tonight, we can never expect to win, regardless of who we're playing, especially in our district. On top of that, when we don't hustle for every loose ball, for every rebound, for every opportunity to deflect a pass, we *deserve* to lose—it's just that simple. Play stupid, play lazy, lose!" His voice picked up with frustration. "I just don't get it. We talked about accomplishing things together, as a team. We talked about persevering through tough times. We talked about the hard work you've all put into this game, about being leaders. And this . . . this is what we get: another halfhearted, unfocused, selfish effort." He stopped for a moment and, staring at the floor, took a deep breath. Then he looked up at the team. "Guys, I've said it before and I'll say it again: We need someone to step up and lead this team, to say enough is enough. We need someone to *lead*, for God's sake! Somethin's gotta give. Somethin's gotta change!" With that he turned and angrily stomped out of the locker room, frustrated as ever.

A single ray of sunshine peeked through the blinds and shined squarely in Coach Rocker's eye as he sat sleeping on the chair in his den. He was still wearing his shirt and tie from the night before. It had been another late night of breaking down film and second-guessing for Coach, and he was teetering on the brink of depression. As he lay there half awake, he battled thoughts of a wasted season. It seemed nothing worked right anymore. Everything Coach had learned over his twenty years in coaching could be thrown out the window. Even the concept of leading with the heart wasn't working.

All week he tried to be more encouraging and more patient. Before the game, he had even reminded his team of the reasons why they played the game—all reasons more important than just winning. This is what leading with the heart was all about . . . he thought. Still, for some inexplicable reason, things seemed to be spiraling downward at an uncontrollable pace.

As he sat up and began to rub the sleep out of his eyes,

Brandon walked in with a cup of coffee. "Thought you might need this, Dad," said Brandon, handing his dad the cup.

"Thanks, buddy. That's thoughtful of you."

"Sorry about the game last night." Brandon sensed the lingering sting from the night before. "Brandon . . . can I ask you a question?"

"Sure, Dad," Brandon replied, plopping down on the couch beside him.

"Why do you think I coach basketball?"

"Whaddya mean 'why'?" asked Brandon, perplexed.

"I mean, why do you think Daddy gets up every morning and goes to the school to teach and coach basketball?" answered Coach, trying his best to simplify the question for his son.

"Well . . . I guess because you like it, and you have fun at it, especially when you win," said Brandon confidently. Coach sat and thought for a moment about Brandon's answer.

"That's it, huh?" quipped Coach. "Because I like it and have fun when I win? That's why you think I coach?"

Brandon shrugged his shoulders. "Yeah . . . I think so. I mean, I don't *know* . . . that *seems* like why you do what you do."

"Interesting," muttered Coach, "interesting." Brandon jumped up from the couch.

"You want to go out and shoot some hoops, Dad?" he asked, a burst of hopeful enthusiasm in his voice.

"Not now, Brandon. I need to gather my thoughts a bit this morning. Not to mention I need to prepare for this morning's practice. Lord knows I need to change something." With a sigh of disappointment, Brandon turned and headed toward the door to spend time with his most loyal companion: his basketball.

Coach couldn't get Brandon's answer out of his head. *Because I like it . . . because it's fun to win?* His mind boggled at the thought. Those weren't the real reasons. He had spent his entire career pouring his heart and soul into the lives of young men . . . and yet, that's what his son saw? He shook his head in disappointment as he pulled out his notes to prepare for the day's practice and tried to shift the gears of his mind.

What could he possibly do to spark a change on this team? What was it that they needed to see to understand what was really important? His mind raced as he jotted down the schedule of drills he planned to run the team through that afternoon. Then, after writing down three or four things they needed to go through, Coach ripped the paper out of the notepad, crinkled it up, and threw it away. None of these things mattered if they didn't make a heartfelt change. And now, what could he possibly do? After racking his brain for the next hour or so, he decided to head into the gym early, hoping for some inspiration along the way.

Walking through the school on Saturday mornings was always a lonely experience, but for some reason, today the hallway seemed especially quiet. As Coach opened the door to his office, he noticed a small, white envelope lying on his desk. *That's strange,* he thought. *That wasn't there last night after the game . . . Who was in my office?* Then it hit him: Joe. Joe had the keys to all the offices. It had to be Joe. He grabbed the envelope and opened it. Inside the envelope, handwritten in big, bold letters across the center of the paper were the words, *"Hang in there, Coach! There's a reason for everything . . . but everything must start with you! Your friend, Joe."*

Coach's thoughts went back to the words Joe had left him with following yesterday's early morning session, the words he'd yelled down the hall to him. "Everything starts with you." Coach read the words aloud to himself again. *With me . . . isn't that kind of the opposite of what we've been talking about?* He shook his head in bewilderment.

This was all becoming too confusing. *My heart's in the right place. I do what I do for the right reasons. I think so, anyway. Hmmm . . . maybe I don't even know what the right reasons are after all. Who knows anymore . . .* For the next two hours Coach sat in his office, struggling to focus on the task at hand. Just a few days earlier he'd thought he had this whole *why* thing figured out, but now, based on how he was feeling, it seemed obvious this was not the case.

By noon Saturday's practice had come and gone without incident. The guys, still pained by the loss the night before, practiced hard but understandably struggled a bit due to the lingering thought of a season of failures. No one was stepping up, and Coach still couldn't figure out why. Although he tried his best to lead from the heart, it was still very clear to him—and the players, too—that something was still missing. He just couldn't quite put his finger on it.

Unfortunately, the next week brought with it more of the same struggles. Despite that the Knights won both their Tuesday and Friday night games, the team played poorly in both outings, winning by one point and three points to teams they'd crushed the year prior.

It was eating Coach up inside. His newfound heart tactics seemed to continue to fail him. Although he felt he had to bring out the hatchet a couple of times, he tried his best all week to lead the team from the heart—encouraging, smiling, and controlling his outbursts the best he knew how. Something deep inside told him he just had to keep trying. But in the end, the guys still struggled with the things they'd been dealing with all season: they lacked the *will* to win, *love* for each other, and the *passion* to play the game.

Chapter 14

Never Too Late

Sitting in his office after practice the following Monday, Coach heard a knock on his door.

"Can I come in, Coach?" a familiar voice rang out from behind the door. It was David Kelton.

"What's up, Muhammad Ali?" Coach joked, making light of the cast David wore on his hand after his locker punch.

"Definitely not my jump shot—yet, that is." They both chuckled as David sat down in front of Coach's desk. "Coach, can I ask you a serious question?" David asked, obviously a bit nervous about what he was thinking.

"Sure. Shoot away," answered Coach. "As long as you don't ask me anything about my criminal record." Again Coach joked, trying to ease David's nervousness.

David started in. "Coach . . . you asked me a question a few weeks ago—you know, when I was working out in the morning—about why I played the game of basketball."

"Yeah, I remember the conversation," said Coach.

"Well, my answers, at the time—they were . . . they were selfish, and I . . . I realize that now. I was focused on getting my touches first. You know, so I could live up to all the hype about this season. I wanted to win—really bad. I mean *really* bad." David's voice quivered as he struggled to find the right words to describe what he was feeling. "But I also wanted to make sure I was leading us . . . in points and rebounds, too. After all, it's my senior year and, well . . . I felt I'd put in my time and thought I deserved it. Now, after having spent a few weeks on the bench watching my teammates and missing the heart of my senior season . . ." David paused as his eyes began to well up with tears. "I guess I see things a bit differently. Coach, my heart . . . it's gone through a real change—I mean a *deep* change, Coach—and I . . . I want to apologize first for my selfishness, for my selfishness in what my focus was deep down in my heart, for my selfishness with my overall attitude, and for my selfishness in hitting the locker. A loss of self-control like that is never acceptable for a leader, and I know that now. I was only thinking about myself. Now I realize that not only are my teammates paying for my selfishness, but through my example, someone else could've decided that my action was acceptable and duplicated it, hurting himself as a result. Well, anyway, as a leader I take full responsibility for my actions, and I'm deeply sorry."

Coach, stunned by his senior's level of maturity, paused before responding. "I appreciate that, David. And I'm really proud that you've recognized these things. I think back to my own playing days, especially in high school. I was never mature enough to recognize any of these things, let alone mature enough to *apologize* for them." Coach seemed almost embarrassed at the thought. "So . . . you mentioned that you wanted to ask me a question, too, David."

"Yeah, Coach, I do." David shifted nervously in his chair. "Coach, when you asked me why I played, I didn't really know. But now, after some deep conversations with a friend . . . now I do know. I know that I play, or *will* play, for a much deeper reason than I ever had before. I know it's no longer just about me. It's much, much bigger than that." David paused and looked down at the floor before continuing on. "But, Coach, I guess . . . I guess I just need to know why you do what you do. Why do you coach?" As he finished the question, he looked straight into the eyes of his coach.

Adjusting uneasily now in his seat, Coach began to speak. "Well . . . first of all, David, because I care about you and your teammates, and I want you all to become successful young men. And next, I guess because I'm passionate about the game of basketball and all that it has to offer you guys in terms of learning opportunities." Coach paused as if there was more. "And then . . . then, I guess, because I love the competition and the thrill of victory after a hard-fought battle. Yeah. Those are the main reasons."

David looked up at him with a look of disappointment. "Coach, I think that sounds great. And I can appreciate all of those things; but, to be honest with you—and please, Coach, don't take offense to this, because I have the utmost respect for you as a person and as my coach—but to most of us on the team . . . it doesn't seem like those are the *real* reasons. Especially not in that order."

Coach felt his face flush as an immediate rush of emotion came over him. *How can he accuse me of lying?* he thought angrily. But he caught himself before overreacting to this perceived accusation. "David . . . I'm not sure I understand what you're saying. Can you help me out here?" said Coach, with a look more confused than angry.

"Coach, if you truly cared about us as young men over everything else you say, you would never have let Brant quit the team."

Coach sat back in his chair and clasped his hands together,

resting them on his stomach. Relieved by what David had just said, he was confident he could defend himself through this one. "Uh, David, Brant quit at one of the toughest points of the season. He bailed out on us. I can't make decisions like that for anyone. He came in with his mind already made up. I'm not going to get down on my knees and beg anyone to stay on this team. Anyone," said Coach, with conviction in his voice.

"I understand, Coach, but do you understand what was going on with Brant outside of basketball?"

Coach froze as, again, he felt his face go flush. "David, he said things were tough at home. I can't help that; things are tough for *all* of us at home, especially when we're losing . . . and—"

"Coach," David interrupted him now, speaking with conviction of his own. "Brant's parents were going through a divorce. Brant was stuck in the middle, trying to take care of his two younger siblings while also trying to deal with his own emotions over the split. Brant's relatives all live in California. He has no family in this area. No adults in his life that could help him through it. I spent hours with Brant trying to encourage him through that time. And you, Coach . . . you never even asked him what was going on at home, let alone try to help him through it. How can you say that your number-one reason for coaching is because you care about us?"

David's voice was filled with emotion now as he thought about the pain his friend had gone through. "With all due respect, Coach—and I think I speak for the rest of the team, too—winning, and all that comes with it, seems to be your number-one priority, your number-one reason for coaching.

That's our perception, anyway. And, Coach, I've always been taught our perception is our reality."

David stood up as if preparing to leave. "I'm sorry, Coach, but I had to get that off my chest. If you want me to leave the team after today, I'll understand why. But I just had to share that with you." David turned and slowly walked out the door.

Coach sat at his desk in shock. Over the last five minutes, he'd run through what seemed like the entire gamut of emotions: from anger, to disbelief, to confusion, and finally now, to deep remorse. *What is wrong with me?* he wondered. *How could I have been so blind? Have I truly been lying to myself this whole time, basically living a life of self-deceit?* Joe's whole heart principle had struck a deep chord in him. And it had made sense. But why was it that no matter how hard he tried, his deepest motive still seemed to be his drive to win, his treasure?

Sitting in the silence of his office, Coach was overcome by the horrible thoughts of his own selfishness. What was this really all about? Why did he coach? Why did he want to be a leader—or more importantly, *why did he even exist?* The thought paralyzed him. *What was God really thinking when he made me?* "Obviously not much," he whispered to himself, holding his face in his hands and shaking his head in disbelief at the emptiness he was now feeling.

Then it came to him. "Joe. Joe!" he said. "That's who I need to talk to—Joe."

At 4:55 the next morning, after another nearly sleepless night, Coach was sitting on the floor by Joe's office, waiting eagerly for his arrival. And sure enough, at 5:00 on the nose, Joe walked around the corner.

"Good morning, my friend!" said Joe, a bit startled to find Coach sitting by his door. "Is everything all right?"

"Yeah . . . well, kinda. Well, you know what? To tell you the truth, no, things are not all right." Coach fumbled with his words as he tried his best to be completely honest with himself and Joe now.

"Well, come in. Let's get some coffee brewing and see if we can figure it all out."

Joe set his bag of books on his desk and walked over to turn the coffee pot on. "So what's going on, Coach?"

"Joe, I can't do it. I mean, I can't lead with the heart." The deep frustration was clear in Coach's voice. "I tried, and I failed. Flat-out, I failed! I'm the biggest loser I know. I have had more success in high school coaching than any of my peers, and yet I'm a failure because I have no clue *why* I do what I do. I mean, I thought I knew. I thought it was for the right reasons. But my guys . . . they see it differently. And my son . . . he sees it differently, too. And you know what? When I search deep within my own heart, I know they're right. I coach 'cause I'm a fierce competitor. I want to win, I fear failure, I need to be in control, and I'm addicted to the rush I get from my successes. My identity is firmly planted in my success as a coach. All the stuff we talked about? That's me. And I don't . . . I don't—" Coach struggled to get the words out as he choked up—"I don't have a clue how to change it." Joe listened to Coach and nodded as if he knew exactly what he was experiencing.

"Not only do I not know why I coach anymore, I guess I don't even know why I'm here on this earth." Coach dropped his head and buried his face in his hands.

After a few moments of silence, Joe spoke up. "Coach . . .

you know all our talks about leading with the heart and about how answering the question *why* is the starting point to all of that?"

Coach nodded.

"And you know how we talked about everything being centered on relationships?" Again Coach gave an affirming nod.

"Well, I have always said, there's only *one way* to really live out your purpose in what you do, and that's to commit to living out your *reason* for existence first."

Joe leaned in and put a hand on Coach's shoulder. "Coach, God created you for him. As the Creator of the entire universe, he has that privilege. But he loves you so much, he gives you a choice to either put your faith in him and build the foundation of your life on his love, or to try to go it alone. It's a good thing to go through this life with a purpose centered on impacting others in a positive way or even on achieving excellence. But what happens eventually is, without a foundation built upon a relationship with him, our hearts succumb to the ways of this world. We approach things in life with a short-term perspective. In other words, we think in terms of our life span on this earth instead of eternally."

Joe got up, walked over to the coffee maker, and continued as he poured two cups of coffee. "When we commit to the purpose of our existence first, our thinking shifts from an earthly perspective to a heavenly, or eternal, perspective. St. Paul talked about this in Romans when he told the church not to conform to the patterns of the world anymore, but to 'be transformed by the renewing of your mind. Then you will be able to test and approve what God's *will* is . . .' Get it? God's purpose for us. That's what he's talking about. We can't truly live this way if we're, in our minds and hearts, focused on what the world tells us success is. Instead, we must focus on what *true* success is, as God defines it in his Word. And everything—I mean *everything*—must be pursued in alignment with that thought process, that intent. Believe me: we all slip up on this from time to time. But in the end, this should be the ultimate driver. The *heart* of everything we do."

Joe handed Coach his cup of coffee and sat down. "Remember, Coach, you can be the best businessman, teacher, coach, preacher, singer, or whatever on this earth and still only be living out a *part* of the purpose you were designed for. Because if all of *that* is not built on the foundation of what your Creator created you for first—to glorify him in your life through your love for him and for others—you will, I repeat, *will* ultimately fail to be your best in this life. Not necessarily in the eyes of the world, but deep inside, whether young, in mid-life, or in old age, you'll feel it in your heart, an emptiness that can only be filled by having a genuine relationship with him and by building everything on that foundation."

Joe picked up the model jet sitting on his desk. "Remember the jet, Coach? Its designer created it to transport people safely to their destinations. It can fly a million times from point A to point B, but if it doesn't fulfill the purpose it was truly created for—flying *people* safely to their destinations—it falls short." Joe set the model back down and sat quietly.

After what seemed like an eternity, Coach began to speak. "I think I get it. I can have the best intentions imaginable. I can positively impact hundreds of people's lives, have a ton of success. I can even come to grips with why I do what I do every day—you know, striving for the second half of my purpose. But in the end, if the foundation, or the first half of my purpose, is not built on my relationship with God, then at some point, *I'll fall short*—period." Coach's voice trailed off as he reflected on his life. "And that is exactly why, even though I bought into the whole leading with the heart concept and thought I clearly answered the question *why,* things still seemed to come up short, even when we won."

"I'm afraid you're right, Coach," said Joe. "You can never really be your best when you're only living out part of your purpose. You have to set the foundation first, then everything must flow out from there."

"Lord knows I've definitely not been the *best* I could be . . . especially these past eight weeks. Come to think of it, even in past seasons when I had all the successes in the world, I wasn't being the best I could be."

Joe waited a few moments before responding. "Coach, *you* are the leader of your team. Not only as the most influential person in the group, but by your formal position, too. And with that position comes great responsibility. You must understand that your actions reflect what's really in your heart . . . your deepest motives, all the time. What's more, your actions, and therefore your heart, can have an incredible influence on the actions and hearts of those you lead.

"Coach, do you know who's responsible for David hitting a locker in a fit of rage?" Joe asked.

"David, of course. He controls his own actions." Coach answered confidently.

"Well, that's partially true . . . but Coach, have you ever displayed a loss of self-control in front of your guys? I mean, have you ever kicked something or thrown something, maybe in hopes of sending a message?"

As if hit squarely between the eyes, Coach immediately

looked away from Joe and sighed guiltily. "Gosh . . . I never really looked at it that way, Joe. I did influence that reaction—in a big way. It's partially my fault David's missed the majority of his senior year. Come to think of it, it's my fault the guys have acted so selfishly this season, too. The reality is, I've modeled selfishness to them all year.

"When Brant quit the team, I was so focused on myself and how angry I was at him, I barely noticed the hurt he was dealing with. I never even asked him about what was going on at home. I had no idea his mom and dad were divorcing. I, of all people—I went through that as a kid, and it was the most devastating experience of my life! Watching my parents split up felt like my own life was being ripped in two. To think that one of my guys was going through that, and I didn't know or even care . . ."

Coach stood up, unable to contain the emotion of the moment. "And now . . . now I think about how I've treated my own family, where *they've* fallen on the list of my priorities. Brandon, my daughter Kylee, even Kathy . . . I've been a horrible dad this whole season, all in pursuit of my own interests, my own 'purpose.' No wonder when I looked at my players, I felt surrounded by selfish boneheads. That's exactly who *I've* been to them all season.

"I think I finally get it. This is what you've been trying to tell me all year. It all starts with me and my leadership . . . my *heart*. The *reason* thing. It all starts with *me:* why *I* exist and why *I* do what I do! I have to live it out. I just wish I could turn back the clock! I mean, I wish I would get another chance . . . but it seems like it's just too late."

"Too late for what?" Joe asked.

"Too late in the season to change things now. Districts start next weekend."

"Coach—" Joe shifted into a fatherly tone—"it's *never* too late to do the right thing. Never too late to get your heart right, as long as you're still breathing."

Jumping up from his seat, Coach looked at his watch. "You're right. I can still do the right thing. I've gotta get ahold of Brant. I mean I have to get ahold of him *now!* I want him back at practice tonight, 'cause I'm gonna lay everything on the line to the guys. They deserve at least that from me before we end this mess of a season."

Practically tripping over his own feet, Coach headed out the door and down the hallway. Then, suddenly, he stopped. He turned and ran back to the open door of Joe's office. "Joe," Coach struggled to catch his breath from the run. "You'll never know what an incredible impact you've made on my life. Thanks . . . thanks, my friend!" Joe gave an acknowledging nod and smiled from behind his desk.

Chapter 15

Reconciliation—A Real Gut Check

Pulling his cell phone out of his pocket, Coach started dialing Brant's number. After a couple of rings, a sleepy voice came across the line.

"Hello?"

"Brant?"

"Yeah . . . uh . . . Coach?" Brant replied, surprised.

"Brant, sorry to wake you up, but . . . I need to talk to you face-to-face, before school today. Is that possible?"

"Uh . . . yeah, sure, I guess. I can be there in a half hour," Brant said, obviously still trying to wake up.

"Great! Uh, Brant? This really is Coach Rocker. This is not a dream. So I'll see you in thirty, right?"

"Yeah, Coach. I'm up. I promise . . . I'll be there."

Coach closed his phone and flipped the light switch on in his office. *I have to get this right . . .* he thought as he sat down and prepared what he would say to Brant. *But it has to start in my own heart first.* Coach bowed his head and began to whisper a prayer. "God . . . I've been such a bonehead. Please forgive me for being so self-centered, for always focusing on my own agenda over everything and everybody else . . . especially you. I need you to be the center of my life, the foundation of my purpose. Help me to live and lead for you above all else. Amen."

At around 6:30, Brant walked through the doorway of Coach's office. "Brant! Am I glad to see you! Please come in, sit down," said Coach.

Brant sat down and tilted his head, looking bewildered. "Yeah, Coach. Nice to see you, too. What's up?" asked Brant, still clueless to what was happening.

"Brant, before I say anything else, I want to say from the bottom of my heart, I'm sorry. That's the very first thing I owe you. Now, I owe you an explanation of what I'm sorry about and why." Brant leaned back in his chair, still shocked at the words coming from his former coach's mouth.

"I have been extremely selfish this season. In my heart, my focus has been on the wrong things, on my own agenda. And nowhere was this more evident than in how I dealt with you and your situation. You deserved better. I had no idea what you were going through in your life. I'm terribly ashamed to say it, but at the time, I really didn't care. Fact is, I went through what you're going through now with your parents when I was twelve, and it devastated me—scarred me for the rest of my life." Brant stared at the floor, shaken by the reminder of the magnitude of what he was facing. "No kid should have to go through that, especially alone, without any adult by their side. God put you in my life for a reason . . . and I blew it. I really, selfishly blew it. Well, almost blew it, 'cause now, I want you back in my life. And I want you on this team.

"I've finally realized what a friend of mine has been try-ing to get through to me for the last two months. This lead-ing from the heart thing—leading with a *purpose*—it has to start with me, as the leader, making a genuine commitment to lead for the right reasons, reasons that will outlast us all. And reasons that align with why we were even created in the first place. Brant, I've finally realized, I need to lead for a deeper reason . . . I need to lead . . . for *God's* sake! And *that* is what I intend to do from here on out. I want to be there for you, especially as you walk through this tough time in your life. And I want you to have your teammates there for you, too. There are only a few weeks, tops, left in the season, but it's never too late to do the right thing. So that's what I'm trying to do right now. You belong on this team, Brant . . . because you're part of this family."

Coach walked around the front of his desk and stood in front of Brant. "Whaddya say, buddy?"

Brant looked up at him, tears streaming down his face. "Yeah, Coach. Yeah . . . I forgive you, and you can count me in."

With that, Coach hugged Brant as a flood of emotions spilled out of the deeply wounded seventeen-year-old. Brant let go, stepped back from his Coach, and began wiping the tears from his eyes.

"I'm sorry, Coach. I'm such a wuss . . . You just can't imagine what I've—"

"What you've been going through? Yes, Brant, I can. And I know it hurts really bad. But you know what? That's what I'm here for from now on. A shoulder to cry on, who knows what you're going through, 'cause I remember that pain like it happened yesterday. But we'll get through it. Oh, and by the way, you're not a wuss, either. If you were, I wouldn't want you back on the team."

They both laughed as Coach grabbed a tissue from his desk drawer and handed it to Brant. "Thanks, Coach . . . Thanks. I promise, I won't let you down again."

"Brant, I let *you* down. And I promise I won't do *that* ever again." Brant gathered up his books and headed out the door. "Three thirty practice, Brant. Don't be late!" Coach yelled as Brant walked down the hall.

"I'll be there!" replied Brant.

As he sat back down in his desk chair, Coach looked at his watch to see how much time he had before first hour. *Just enough time to call Kathy!* he thought to himself, dialing her cell number. He couldn't wait to talk to his wife about what had happened and about how he was determined to make changes at home as a result. Unfortunately, the stress level in the household had always intensified the week of districts— and this year more than in the past. So Kathy took the kids to stay at her parents' farm a few miles out of town and planned to avoid her husband until Friday night's game. Assuming there was one, of course.

After four rings the call went into her voicemail. Not wanting to leave a message regarding such an important subject, Coach clicked his phone off. *I really need to talk to her. I need to apologize to her and tell her how I've changed. Actually, I need to* show *her I've changed.* After thinking about it for a few more minutes, Coach knew a simple phone call wouldn't suffice. This was a conversation that needed to happen face-to-face, so as important as it was, he knew it would have to wait until she was back in town on the weekend. He prayed it would keep until then.

Chapter 16

Influence and Responsibility

By the time 3:30 rolled around, the guys had gathered at the end of the gym, prepared to begin their normal prepractice warm-up routine. But today was different. Walking out on the gym floor, Coach blew his whistle and summoned everyone to follow him into the locker room. As they filed in one by one, they noticed Brant sitting alone on the bench in front of the whiteboard. Surprised to see him, most of the guys greeted him with a fist bump while a couple of them hugged him, still unsure what he was doing there in the first place. On the board was a simple drawing of a stick man with a hatchet in one hand and a basketball with a W drawn on it in the other. Coach walked to the front of the room and stood beside the whiteboard.

"Guys, today is going to be a little different than normal. I have a number of things I want to share with you, so I'm not sure if we'll even make it back onto the court. But frankly, that's not the most important thing right now, anyway, so I'd ask that you open up your minds and hearts to me for the next hour or so while I share a few things I've learned over the past few months." The guys exchanged glances of confusion back and forth, perplexed by what was happening.

"Over the years in my career as a coach, I've had more success, in terms of wins, than any other high school coach in the state of Kentucky. And as a coach and leader, my philosophy has always centered on two main methods of motivation. First, on winning, which is represented by the W you see in this guy's hand. Next, when that wasn't enough—in other words, when guys got selfish or lazy on me—I brought out the hatchet and scared them into submission." A few of the guys chuckled and nodded in agreement, recalling some of their recent experiences in practice. "But men, over the last couple of days, really over the last two months, with the help of a great friend, you guys have opened my eyes to a new reality that I've been missing all along.

"You see, you guys became selfish, greedy, arrogant, bitter, angry, and resentful. And on top of all that, you lost your *will* to win, your *love* for each other, and your *passion* to play the game." He wrote the three terms beside the stick man, then turned back to the team. "And that, in a nutshell, is why we've lost all the games we have this season."

With his head down, Billy Conner leaned toward David and whispered, "Here we go again. The 'no leadership' speech." David smirked in agreement.

But then Coach sat down on a stool in front of the team and dropped his head as he began to speak softly. "But, guys . . . here's the real reason I brought you in here today. You need to know that this mind-set, this way of thinking I just described to you, has been my fault . . . and I owe each one of you a personal apology for it. So, Billy, I'm sorry. David, I'm sorry . . ." Coach continued around the room, calling each player by name and giving him a personal apology.

"I also want you to know the specifics of where I've gone wrong this season and why this is my fault. First, as the leader of this team, I've been a model of complete selfishness. Although I told you guys that the reason I was here was to help you all become successful young men, I was not really willing to do that at the expense of losing. In other words, even though that was, and still *is,* a big part of the reason I do what I do, winning has really been the most important thing to me, followed by things like control and the attention that the success of winning brings with it. Those were the *whys* at the heart of my coaching. If I could teach you some good lessons along the way, great; that would be a bonus, and that's what I would hide behind as my 'purpose' for coaching. But the reality was, in my heart, my motives were self-centered. I proved this again and again at different points in the season. But nowhere was this more evident than in how I handled the situation with one of your teammates, Brant.

"Most all you guys know what Brant is going through right now. And I can tell you from personal experience, it's flat-out hell. But when Brant came to me to quit the team, all I could think about was me and how his decision would make it harder for us to win. I didn't ask him what was going on at home, or if I could help him in any way—perfect proof that my priorities and my purpose for coaching really *weren't* centered on the right things. So, I messed up big time, and I apologized to Brant this morning and asked him to rejoin us on the team. Gentlemen, make no mistake: this is not about helping us win more games as we head into our district playoffs. No, this is about all of us helping someone we genuinely care about get through a tough time. That's what real teammates do for each other. So, Brant . . . welcome back, buddy."

In an instant the whole team cheered and swarmed Brant with hugs and pats on the back. They all knew what he'd been through and welcomed the chance to bring him back on board.

After settling the team down a bit, Coach hopped off the stool he was sitting on. "Guys, the next thing I have to apologize for is David's broken hand." A few of the guys shot strange looks back and forth wondering how *he* was responsible for the accident. Coach turned and wrote the words LEADERSHIP: INFLUENCE + RESPONSIBILITY on the whiteboard above the stick man.

"Guys, responsibility is a huge part of effective leadership. As a leader, you're always influencing those around you, through words and actions. And with this influence comes responsibility—not only for your formally assigned duties as a leader, but also for how you influence others as they approach their assigned duties, too.

"Billy," Coach called out his senior point guard. "What are some of your assigned duties on the floor?"

"I'm supposed to run the offense, play good defense, and bring the ball up the floor. Be kinda the floor general," answered Billy.

"Right. Those are all specific duties you've been assigned, your formal responsibilities," said Coach. "Now let's look at some responsibilities more closely related to your influence. What if every time you turned the ball over, you blamed one of your teammates; or if every time there was a bad call, you ripped into the official. How would your teammates react?"

Billy thought for a second. "Some would probably get on me about it."

"Okay . . . how else?"

"Some would start jawing back at me?"

"Yeah, right, what else would they do?" asked Coach, trying to get Billy to think beyond the obvious.

"Well, some might begin to think it was okay to blame

others or to rip on the officials, and they may start to act that way, too."

"Exactly!" exclaimed Coach. "They'd be influenced by your actions. And guess what? As a leader on this team, if one of your teammates ends up getting a technical for yelling at a ref after watching you do the same thing for weeks on end, guess who's responsible?"

"Both?" Billy responded hesitantly.

"Right—you're both responsible. Make no mistake, as a senior leader on this team, you're heavily responsible for your influence on the actions and attitudes of your teammates through what you've modeled. So, as a leader, you must always step up to the plate and take full responsibility for your contribution to problems that arise as a result of that influence.

"Guys, I gotta tell you, this is a huge problem in society. Nowadays no one wants to take responsibility for anything. All you have to do is turn on the nightly news to see that play out. Politicians blame other politicians; executives blame the workers; workers blame the executives. Everybody wants to blame everybody else but *no one* wants to take responsibility for their own role in causing the problem!

"Unfortunately, this happens in the home, too. Parents blame the teachers and coaches without ever considering the role their kid may be playing in causing the problem. So what does this teach the kid? Find the fault in others; never consider your own contribution to the problem. We're teaching entire generations to be experts at shirking responsibility." Coach stepped back over to the stool and sat down.

"So, what's my point?" Again, Coach's voice quieted to a whisper. "I'm guilty of shirking my own responsibility for my influence on this team in a big way this season, and I'm sorry.

Throughout this season I've lost control countless times—most notably when I kicked over the Gatorade jug. So, when David lost control and punched a locker, I myself, as the leader of this team, was significantly responsible for his actions. My own unacceptable actions influenced his behavior."

Unable to contain himself, David blurted out, "Wait a minute, Coach. I punched the locker; it was my fault."

"Don't get me wrong, David. You made a poor choice, too. And you're responsible for that choice. But as I said, guys, I screwed up as the leader of this team. I was a bad influence, so I'm responsible too, and I'm sorry. I'm really, really sorry."

The team sat in silence, not knowing what to say as their coach humbly stood before them, apologizing for his actions. This display of remorse and humility was something none of them had ever experienced with one of their coaches, especially not one as successful as Coach Rocker. It was obvious by the looks on their faces that this moment would have a deep, lasting impact on each and every one of them.

Coach hopped back off the stool, picked up a marker, and turned to the whiteboard. "Men, the last thing I want to share with you is the reason I've made the changes I've made. And this is really important, because the fact of the matter is, if I stood up here telling you these things with a hidden agenda in my heart, with my own secret aspirations of success at the forefront of my mind, I'd be doing it for all the wrong reasons, even if I said all the right things. Instead, guys, I want you to know that I've had a deep change of heart. And by that I mean I've finally recognized the importance of why I do what I do every day . . . not just as a coach, but as a man put here on this earth for a reason . . . a *purpose.*"

Coach wrote the word WHY off to the side and then

drew a big heart at the center of the stick man. "*This,*" Coach pointed to the heart. "This is where everything must begin. Not here or here." Coach pointed to the hatchet and then the W. Next, he drew a line with an arrow between the word WHY and the heart.

"You see, guys, over the course of my career I've had more success, in the eyes of the *world,* than any other high school coach in Kentucky basketball history . . . and yet, in spite of that, the reality is I've been failing. Not necessarily in the eyes of the public or my friends, or even myself, because society measures success or failure in wins and losses—on paper anyway. That's what they'll always tell you counts. How much money you have or what title you earn or how big a house you live in or what kind of car you drive or, yeah, how many championships you've won. That's how society will measure you to determine whether you're a success or a failure. But the fact of the matter is that measuring stick leaves out one giant factor, the most important factor: *who you are versus who you were created to be.*"

Coach paused to let the thought sink in for a few seconds, then began again. "I thought I knew who I was. I thought I knew why I did what I did, too. Of course, I wanted to make men out of boys. I wanted to teach young men how to fight, to persevere, to work hard, to work together, to sacrifice for their teammates, to be self-disciplined, to be successful leaders. All very good things, but guys, these things, in and of themselves, miss the main point in life. And thanks to some friends of mine who cared enough to help me recognize this, I've finally seen the light. Despite all the championships, all the worldly successes, unless I'm living *every day* in true alignment with who I was created to be, I'm not being the best I can be. So in a way, I'm failing, because that purpose is meant to be the very foundation from which everything else flows in my life. That's how God designed it. Unless we build our lives on the right foundation, we'll never, I repeat *never* realize what it means to be the best we can be."

Coach turned back to the board and wrote the word PURPOSE at the center of the heart. Then to the side he wrote the word PRAYER. "Guys . . . you were created by God for a reason centered on relationship. He loves you and wants to have a relationship with you. That's where everything starts. Don't get caught up in all the rules and guidelines you think he's set in place to make your life miserable. And don't get caught up in thinking you can earn your way to God either. You can't."

Again, Coach pointed to the hatchet and the W. "Plain

and simple, God loves you and wants you to love him. Your acceptance of and commitment to his gift of love must be your foundation in life. Everything else must flow from that."

Directly under the word PRAYER he wrote the words EMBRACE POSITION. "This is where you are today. You're on this team, you're in high school, you're part of a family. So you know what? Embrace it! Quit focusing so much on where you'll be next year or how you can become this great . . . fill in the blank. Commit to living out your purpose today, being the best you can be right where you are."

"Uh . . . Coach," interrupted Billy with a puzzled look on his face. "I don't get it. Do you mean we should give up on our dreams?"

"Absolutely not, Billy. Our dreams and passions are an important part of our lives. But they can also destroy us if we become so focused on them that we forget to live out our purpose right where we are. Fact is, guys, we are called to be our very best in everything we do ... everything.

"You are where you are for a reason. You can either learn to embrace it and be your best or reject it and drag your feet through the rest of your life. The only problem with the latter approach is God may just want to see what you can do where you are, before he trusts you to go where you want to be." Billy sat back in his chair and nodded.

Next, Coach wrote the words LOVE PEOPLE under EMBRACE POSITION. "Men, look around you. These guys are in your life for a reason. Think about your families, your classmates, teachers, friends—they're all in your life, waiting for you to recognize that they're a key part of your purpose. God put them there for a reason. What are you going to do about that? Relationships lie at the center of your purpose.

They should be a major driving force behind everything you do. Never forget, pursuing anything at the expense of key relationships in our lives takes us out of being our absolute best—our best as defined by our Creator."

Unable to resist the opportunity, David chimed in. "Mr. Taylor really helped me on this one, Coach. The whole *people* thing . . . I never really saw my role with my teammates as anything more than just, well, being a teammate. But he taught me to look beneath the surface, to really listen to what's going on in the hearts around me, to recognize the deeper needs of my teammates, and the other people God has put in my life, too. When we do that, we begin to see that they really are there for a reason, a reason central to our purpose."

"That's great, David! You're exactly right," said Coach. "Just think what it'd be like if we all lived our lives like that. Valuing each and every person we encounter as if they truly were a central part of our purpose, as if the opportunity to positively impact a life was a gift from God that each of us could give to others endlessly." Coach looked at his guys excitedly at the thought of what he had just described.

Turning back to the whiteboard he wrote the words SET PRIORITIES under LOVE PEOPLE. "Guys, this is another one I've missed big time. I've blown it with my own family over the years. Brandon's ten and Kylee's six, and they both barely know me as anything other than a basketball coach. Is that really who I am, or who I should be to them . . . or to my wife? Your priorities need to be right if you're to truly live out your purpose and be the *best* you can be."

Brant caught Coach's eye. The topic had obviously touched a nerve. "You're not the only parent who's blown this one, Coach," said Brant. "After listening to my mom and dad fight for the past three months, I think they both had this area screwed up. And now my brother, sister, and I are all paying for it."

"And that's really sad, Brant," said Coach, easily empathizing. "It's just not right. But when the foundation isn't right, everything else eventually gets out of whack.

"Here's the thing, guys. Since I've decided to live for the purpose God created me for, from here on, my goal will be to have everything I do flow from the foundation I've established in him. I want God to be at the center of all my priorities. Did ya catch that? No more 'God first, family second, and school, work, or team third'—that's a bunch of crap, as far as I'm concerned. It never works. God's too big to be put in a 'priority' box. Instead, he needs to be at the center of all my priorities in life because he wants to be a part of everything I do. That means whether I'm working on taking care of myself mentally, physically, emotionally, or spiritually, God remains at the center. My relationship with my wife must be number one on my list of priorities, but God must remain at the center of that relationship." Coach paused as he thought of Kathy and how he had yet to talk to her. He missed her desperately and couldn't wait to show her his change of heart.

"Guys, as Brant can attest, you don't have to look very far to find people who've worked their whole lives chasing their own version of 'success' only to leave behind them a trail riddled with casualties from priorities gone awry. Broken families, addictions, failed friendships—the list goes on and on, and it's just not worth it. To truly live out your purpose, your priorities must be right."

Next Coach wrote the words LIVE PASSIONATELY on the whiteboard. Then, he drew an arrow connecting all of the P words with the heart. He stood and looked at the word for a few moments, then turned back to the team.

"Finally, men, you must live with *passion*. Passion is an emotion sparked by the right attitude toward the right pursuits. Sometimes in our society, people wrongly assume your passion is designed to signal to you what you're supposed to pursue in life. If that's the case, I gotta say I'm in trouble, because I'm passionate about a lot of things. Well, a lot of things that are pretty selfishly rooted, and I believe could probably get me into trouble. And I bet you guys are, too." The guys looked at each other, cracking smiles as typical teenage-boy thoughts of fast cars, fast women, and fast money flashed across their minds.

"Fact is, guys, passion is a choice, a choice that should *follow* our commitment to our purpose. Even today, as I've thought more and more about these things, the passion in my gut continues to grow. I *want* to live my life committed to my purpose. I *want* to embrace my position in life, losses and all. I *want* to see the people in my life as I'm supposed to see 'em. And I'm determined from here on to live out the right priorities in my life, too. So now . . . now, I can hardly contain the passion I feel to live every day in the purpose I was created for. Passion must follow purpose, guys, not the other way around!

"Men," Coach stood pointing at the heart in the illustration on the board. "I truly believe being the best you can be all starts right here. Once your heart is right, relationships, priorities, everything falls into place." He drew another arrow toward the words WILL, LOVE, and PASSION. "And the more you guys recognize these things and follow suit, the bigger the heart of our team will get." He put the cap back on the marker he was holding and walked over to an empty spot on the bench beside Brant and sat down.

The players sat silently, each of them studying the illustration their coach had just laid out before them. The looks on their faces made it very clear: the message had sunk in. This was what they were missing all year, and even though they hadn't realized it, this was the change they'd been waiting for.

Coach stood up again. "Guys, we may only have tomorrow night's practice and maybe a game or two left, but I know one thing for sure. No matter what happens, whether we win one, four, or by some miracle of God, we win the state championship, this season will be a success if we all walk away from it with a true grasp of what it means to lead from the heart, for the right reasons. To lead . . . for *God's* sake!"

The clock on the wall read 4:20. "Well, men, we're actually supposed to be outta here tonight by 5:00. So it's up to ou: you want to practice, or call it a night?"

Immediately David jumped up. "Practice, Coach! I mean, I think we need to get out there together and get after it.

'Cause I don't know about you guys, but I don't want to be one and done in districts this year. No way!" Despite his condition, David had continued to be one of the main leaders on the team. He set the tone for practice each day through his example of hard work on the sidelines. So immediately, the rest of the guys began to signal their agreement.

"Yeah, Coach. We need to get Brant back in the flow of things, and quick," said Billy. The team jumped up and circled around Coach.

David spoke up again. "Guys, not Knights tonight. How about 'heart' instead? 'Cause that's what we're all about from here on out. 'Heart' on three. One, two, three!"

"Heart!" the team shouted enthusiastically and broke the huddle to run out to the gym.

Chapter 17

Burying the Hatchet

On his way home from that night's shortened practice, Coach's cell phone rang. Kathy's voice came across the line.

"Steve, saw you called earlier today. Thought I better call back just to make sure everything's okay."

"Everything's great, Kathy. Actually, really great. I just have some important things to tell you. About some changes I'm making in my life. I want to share them with you."

"Really, like what?" Kathy tried to hide her skepticism, but her struggle with her husband's issues was still obvious.

"Well, actually, I think it'd be best if I shared them with you face-to-face."

"Okay, whatever you say, Steve. Just remember we're not coming back till Friday night."

"Yeah, I know. And I understand," said Coach. Despite Kathy's standoffish manner, he was determined to stay positive. "Just know that I'm excited to see ya and miss ya. I love you."

An awkward moment of silence followed. Kathy's frustration had definitely reached a new level. She struggled to respond. "Yeah, Steve . . . love you too," she replied almost begrudgingly. The phone clicked off.

That night's shortened practice and Wednesday night's practice were among the best of the season. But interestingly enough, they were also the toughest. Coach pushed the guys hard and coached more intensely than he had all year. Clearly leading with the heart was not for sissies and was definitely not to be mistaken as the easy way out. But now the guys had truly bought in. They knew beyond a shadow of a doubt *why* their coach was pushing them to their absolute limits, and they understood that he genuinely loved and wanted what was best for each of them. They also now knew why they needed to push themselves to those same limits, too. They understood it was about more than just themselves. They understood that they were accountable to their teammates and had a responsibility to one another to lay it *all* on the line—to give the very best they had for each other, to work at it with *all* their hearts. There was no question: leading with the heart was definitely better, but by no means easier.

The guys had clearly welcomed Brant back into the mix and were beginning to gel as a team. And after practicing at a level of passion not seen since the previous season, the team began to play at that same level too. Both Thursday and Friday nights' games of the district tournament were blowouts. The Knights had finally begun to play like most had expected them to play at the start of the season. But now, with the rematch of the number-ten-ranked Springston Tigers up next for the title game, everyone knew it was going to take a lot more than just emotion to get the job done. Just a little over a month ago, the Tigers had beaten the Knights by three in what at the time looked like an upset. Now the tables were turned as the Tigers had finished the season undefeated in the district and had buzzed through their first two tournament opponents to become the favorite to win Saturday night's Northeastern District Tournament championship. There was no doubt: this would be a true test of where the Knight's actually stood.

Early Saturday morning, Coach snuck into the kitchen to make breakfast for Kathy, who'd returned home the night before. Finally, the opportunity he'd been waiting for had arrived. He was determined to do something special for his wife as a symbol of how serious he was about changing his ways.

Although he tried his best to quietly sneak around the kitchen without waking anyone, the pitter-patter of bare feet scampering across the tiled entryway next to the kitchen was a sure sign he'd failed in his attempt.

"Whatcha doin', Dad?" asked Brandon as he peeked around the corner with Kylee at his side, both still in their PJ's.

"Shhhh . . . I'm going to surprise Mommy."

"Surprise Mommy? Is it her birthday?" Kylee asked, holding her little pink blanket close to her mouth.

"No, silly, it's not Mommy's birthday. But it *is* a special day," said Coach, pulling a carton of eggs out of the fridge.

"What's so special about it?" asked Brandon as he hopped up to sit in his favorite spot on the counter.

"Well, today I'm going to tell Mommy how much I love her and how my heart has changed. And how I'm going to change the way I treat her and the two of you."

"Whaddya mean, Dad?" asked Brandon.

"Yeah, whaddya mean, Daddy?" Kylee asked, echoing her big brother.

"Well, over the past few months I haven't treated any of you like I should've. I put my own agenda, my own personal goals ahead of you guys. In fact, I've put them ahead of a whole bunch of relationships in my life, including my relationship with God. And that's not right. Now, since I'm committed to building everything in my life around my true purpose, I'm determined to focus more on each of you."

"So does that mean we'll get to play basketball together every day?" asked Brandon.

"Well, maybe not every day, Brandon. Dad still has responsibilities he has to uphold in other relationships, too. But you can be sure of this, buddy: your dad is going to spend more quality time with you. So you know what? That definitely means playing more basketball together. And it also means you just might have to tag along with me to practice once in a while."

Brandon jumped down off the counter excitedly. "Are you serious, Dad?"

"Absolutely, bud. And Kylee, this means you and I need to start spending a little more time coloring together, too."

Kylee giggled as both kids tore off to their rooms excited to get dressed for what they believed was truly a new day.

After putting the final touches on the breakfast he'd prepared, Coach crept into the bedroom, hoping to surprise his wife. With tray in hand, he flipped on the light. Startled by the sight, Kathy rolled over and rubbed her eyes in disbelief. She remembered what her husband had told her Tuesday night, about making some changes, but now . . . now *this* was almost too good to be true. She wondered if she was dreaming.

"Good morning, hon. How are ya?" Coach asked, sitting down beside her on the bed.

"Great . . . Are you okay?" asked Kathy.

"I'm great, too. I really am," Coach answered, a reassuring look on his face.

"Well, I'm excited for you. I have to admit, you did seem . . .

well, a bit different at last night's game. Like you were just more . . . more at peace with what you were doing, or maybe even with who you are. I don't know, does that make sense?"

"Absolutely! It makes sense because I *am* different. And because I am, I need you to know something really important."

"Okaaay," Kathy answered hesitantly.

"I need you to know that some of the things you've heard me mention about my conversations with Joe, the janitor I've been meeting with, things about . . . you know, about leadership and purpose? Well, it finally all came together this week. I finally got it. I got what was at the core, the real heart of everything."

"Yeah?"

"Yeah. And in light of that, you need to know that I'm determined to be a better husband and father by putting you guys ahead of winning more as a coach. I've failed in those areas of my life over the past ten years, partially because I took those relationships for granted, but also because I got caught up in the whole *pursuit of success* thing. I didn't understand my true purpose in this life. And because of that, my priorities got out of whack and . . . I'm sorry. I take full responsibility for my failures."

Coach leaned in closer to his wife and looked straight into the beautiful, big, brown eyes he'd hardly noticed over the past three months. "You and the kids are so important to me. I love you guys so much . . . and I want that love to be reflected in my priorities from here on out." He bent down and gently kissed Kathy on the forehead.

She looked up at her husband amazed, but still a bit skeptical. She'd seen him go through changes before, but for some reason, this one seemed different. This one seemed to be from the inside out.

Although he'd been sharing a few things here and there with her about his conversations with Joe, she had no idea they were having so deep an impact on his life. "I . . . I don't know what to say, Steve . . . other than I accept your apology and forgive you. I know you've been under a lot of pressure lately, and I understand that—"

"Please," Coach interrupted. "No excuses for me this time, hon. Seriously, if my priorities were right, the pressure wouldn't have made a difference. I was wrong, period. I had such a passion to compete, to control, to win, that I allowed those things to come before my true purpose in life. I was created to love—love God and others. So naturally, my relationship with you needs to be at the top of my priorities. And of course, my relationship with God needs to be at the center of that."

Kathy laid her head back down on the pillow and sighed. "So you really are serious about this whole purpose thing, huh?" she asked, staring at the ceiling, still in disbelief.

"Oh yeah. Serious, determined, and passionate," Coach responded confidently. "Now enjoy your breakfast, before your eggs get cold and I have to go out and make you new ones."

Kathy laughed at the thought of her husband making her eggs since cooking of any kind was not his specialty. As she sat up to eat her breakfast, the two of them continued to talk over the details of the past months' experiences with Joe and how they'd so deeply affected the heart of the entire team.

The district championship that evening lived up to every expectation and then some. The two teams traded leads back and forth throughout the entire game before Brant's three-pointer knotted the score at 68 with just thirty seconds left. The Knights headed toward the bench after the Tigers called a timeout to set up their offense. As the guys gathered around Coach, David jumped off the bench and into the middle of the huddle.

"Guys, we can do this. This is everything we've been waiting for. We have a chance to lock down on these guys. The last time we played 'em, I punched a locker after the game. Coach and I are both sorry for that one. But you guys . . . you guys have a chance to erase a lot of that pain by getting it done right now. So who's gonna make a play? Who's gonna make the big stop? It's not about me, it's not about you, it's not even about Coach: It's about *us!*"

"You heard him!" affirmed Coach. "This is about us! Now go out there and play defense like never before, so that no matter what happens when the buzzer sounds, you can lay your head on the pillow tonight with no regrets. None! Heart on three. One, two, three!"

"Heart!"

The Tigers inbounded the ball and walked it up the floor as the Knights matched up in a man-to-man pressure defense. Passing the ball back and forth to his teammates by the half-court line, the Tigers' point guard waited until the twelve-second mark to signal for the play to begin. He passed the ball to the right side of the floor to sharpshooter Jurell Swanson, who had almost single-handedly broken the Knights' hearts in the previous match-up between the two teams. Immediately the point guard cut down the middle of the lane, hoping for a backdoor opportunity, given the pressure defense the Knights were applying. Nothing was there. Next, the Tigers' center jumped out to set a ball screen for Swanson. Eight seconds, seven, six . . . Swanson faked right, then came back left, brushing off the right shoulder of the ball screener. It was déjà vu—until Brant, who'd been on the weak side of the lane, sniffed the play out and took a gamble. He lunged forward to tip the ball, and as he did, his fingers grazed the leather just enough to send the ball bouncing toward the other end of the floor. The race was on. Four seconds . . . three . . . two. Brant tipped the ball ahead and sprinted toward his basket. As the final second flashed across the scoreboard, he got both hands on the ball and, from seventeen feet out, stopped, popped, and *swish*, right at the buzzer. The Knights were district champs. The place went nuts!

As Coach watched his players celebrate from the sidelines, his eyesight became blurred with tears of joy. He was so happy for his players, so happy for all they'd learned and all they'd overcome from the previous weeks. They deserved this, and he was thrilled for them. And then he saw something he knew he'd never forget: Brant and David, embracing in the middle of the celebration, stopped and ran out of the center of the crowd and over to the end line. There, standing in the corner, was Joe. The two boys hugged Joe as if he were a long-lost friend. And Joe, as excited as Coach had ever seen him before, hugged them back.

At that moment, Coach began to put the pieces together. Joe had not only impacted his life; he'd also been pouring himself into the lives of both Brant and David. What a special, special man Joe really was, Coach thought, as fans continued to congratulate him on the victory. Then, as he watched the special moment, he caught Joe's eye. He couldn't resist jogging over to join the celebration on the sidelines. The two men embraced like brothers.

After a few moments Joe looked Coach in the eyes, winked, and said like only he could say, "I knew you'd get 'em there, Coach. I knew you'd help 'em find the real reason they do what they do."

Coach, in attempt to emulate his mentor, winked back at Joe and replied, "Thanks, Joe. Thanks, for more than you'll ever know." With that, he turned, and headed to center court for the presentation of the tournament trophy.

Over the next week, practices again went very well as the team prepared for the regional tournament. Although Coach hadn't scheduled any formal time with Joe, he still had a few meaningful chats with him following his practices that week. Joe somehow always found his way into the gym during practice time. He'd stand off in the corner with a notepad or an old book in his hands, making notes to himself as he watched the boys run up and down the floor. In the past, Coach had always wondered why he appeared to care so much about the team. He had always figured he was just a big sports fan. He knew now that Joe was much, much more than that.

Chapter 18

A Real Treasure

As expected, the first two games of the regional tournament were much tougher than the first two games of the district tournament. From the very start, the Knights had their hands full facing back-to-back ranked opponents. Nevertheless, the guys were playing inspired ball now and refused to be denied the chance to continue the pursuit of their newfound purpose, opening the tournament with a four-point victory over East Side. And despite being down by twelve points to Marion Lakes, late in the second half, two three-pointers by Billy Conner sparked a Knight rally that helped them seal a three-point victory in the second game. The stage was set. The Knights would face the number-five-ranked Marshall County Mavericks for a chance to return to the state tournament.

After the Marion Lakes game, the guys walked across the gym floor to shake hands with the opposing team. As usual, Coach glanced down to the sideline, where he'd hoped to find Joe. But, to his surprise, Joe was nowhere in sight. He glanced toward the bleachers where the Knight fans were starting to make their way toward the doors, and still he did not see Joe. Coach had grown quite fond of Joe now and was disappointed at not being able to share the victory with him. After all, Coach knew that Joe was probably more responsible for his team's recent winning streak than anyone besides maybe the players themselves. He was sure Joe wouldn't have missed this game.

The bus, filled with the chatter of happy players, slowly rolled out of the parking lot and headed back east toward Franklin North High School. Feeling good about where they were as a team, the guys were definitely enjoying the ride.

About thirty minutes after leaving the school, Brant came rushing to the front of the bus. "Coach, *Coach!* Joe's in the hospital. He's sick . . . he's very sick . . ."

"What?" Coach tried to settle Brant down. "Calm down, Brant, calm down. Tell me what happened. How do you know?"

"I didn't see him after the game. He's always been there for me after every game, so I got worried and called his house. His son answered . . . said he'd been sick for quite some time, and this morning, he took a turn for the worse."

"Brant, is he okay . . . I mean, is he stable or critical?" Coach asked, trying to keep himself composed despite the shock he was also feeling.

"I think . . . I think he's okay, 'cause his son didn't sound too alarmed, but I guess . . . I don't really know."

"Listen, I'm sure he'll be all right, Brant, and it's too late now to call or visit him yet tonight. Let's try to go see him first thing in the morning. I'll pick you up, say, around 8:30. How does that sound?"

"Okay, Coach. I'll be ready." Brant turned around hesitantly and made his way back to his seat.

The next morning, as Coach turned into Brant's driveway, both Brant and David bounded out the front door. "Hey, guys," said Coach. "I didn't expect to see you here, David."

"Yeah, we were both pretty upset last night about Joe, so

I ended up just crashing here. Didn't want to leave my buddy hangin', ya know," David said, patting Brant on the shoulder. "Besides, Joe's impacted my life in a big way, and I wanted to be part of cheering him up this morning, too."

After a brief stop at the front desk to find out what room Joe was in, the three of them headed toward the elevator to Joe's room. When they arrived, Coach tapped on the door quietly, in case Joe was sleeping.

From inside, a friendly woman's voice called out to them, "Come in!" As they slowly peeked around the door, they saw Joe's wife sitting in a chair beside Joe, who was lying, apparently, asleep on the bed. She smiled in a warm and welcoming way as the three men filed into the room.

"Good morning. You must be Mrs. Taylor," said Coach. "My name is Steve Rocker, and this is David Kelton and Brant Stevens."

"Oh, no need for introductions. I know who you boys are, better than you can imagine," she said in a sweet, motherly fashion. "My Joe fills me in on all the happenings at Franklin North, especially with the basketball team."

Initially appearing to be asleep, Joe opened his eyes when he heard the familiar voices in the room.

"Well, well, well! Congrats, men," Joe said, extending his hand to each of them.

"Joe, we missed you last night," said Coach.

"Yeah, we almost didn't get it done without you there, you know," chimed in David. Joe chuckled and labored a bit as he tried to sit up.

"So what's going on with you, Joe?" asked Coach, concerned.

"Well, I've had this . . . this . . . nagging problem. Nothin' too serious—for the most part, anyway. My liver just hasn't been working quite like it's supposed to. And I just can't seem to get it fixed. Much as I know how to fix most things, I just can't seem to fix this one. Darndest thing, you know, that liver . . . Can't *liver* with it, can't *liver* without it." Joe winked at the guys, cracking up at his own joke. "But hey," Joe pointed his index finger to the sky and instantly got a more serious look on his face, "remember, there's a reason for everything. And I'm not worried. It's happened a couple times before. Usually in here for two or three days, tops. Then they send me on my way again. Feelin' good as ever." Joe flashed the guys his reassuring smile.

"Well, I know one thing," said Brant, "you had me scared half to death last night. It's just not like you to miss a big game like that . . ."

"Yeah," interrupted Joe, "and I'm a little ticked they won't let me outta here for tonight's game either. I know this: I don't plan on missin' the state tournament next weekend. Oh, whoops. Sorry, Coach." Joe shrugged and covered his mouth. "Didn't mean to get the guys looking past your next opponent."

"Ah, don't worry about it, Joe. It's just nice to see you're back to your old self," chuckled Coach. "We were really worried about ya. But hey, seriously, we'll get the win tonight for ya to make sure you get to see the big one next weekend, live." Joe gave the guys a thumbs-up and a reassuring nod.

After visiting with the two of them for another thirty minutes or so, the guys said their good-byes, gave Mrs. Taylor a hug, and headed out the doorway.

No sooner than they'd walked out, Coach heard Joe call out for him. "Coach!" He turned around and poked his head back into the room. "Have I ever showed you this book?" Joe held up a small, raggedy old book about the size of a large wallet. On the cover were four barely legible words: "Lead for God's sake!"

Coach walked back to Joe's bedside to take a little closer look. "Nope, you haven't, Joe . . . or at least not that I recall, and I think I'd remember seeing a book that beat up." Coach couldn't help ribbing his friend just a little at the sight of the worn-out, old book.

"Well, I want you to take it for a while and leaf through it. Outside of the Bible, it's my favorite book. All the stuff we've been talking about—it's all in there, and more."

Coach reached out as Joe handed him the book. "I wondered where you got all your wisdom," joked Coach as he took the book and briefly flipped through a couple of pages. The book was packed with underlines and notes that Joe had made to himself over the years. "Thanks, Joe. This looks great."

"Hey, my pleasure. Enjoy it. Keep it as long as you like, but when you're done with it . . . try to remember to get it back to me. I get lost if I go too long without it." Joe gave Coach one more of his famous winks as Coach turned and walked out the door.

Later that morning, after a brief shoot-around practice with the team, Coach headed home to complete the final preparations for the big game that night. Determined to memorize his opponents' tendencies, he sat glued to the TV with his remote in hand, replaying over and over again the Mavericks' offensive sets.

About an hour into his routine, Coach glanced toward the window and noticed Brandon alone in the driveway shooting baskets. He tried to justify refocusing on the task at hand. *There's no way I can afford to take fifteen minutes with Brandon right now, just hours away from the biggest game of the season.* For the next few seconds he battled the thoughts that so many times in his past had dictated his behaviors. But then, thoughts of the purpose conversations he had had with Joe began to resonate in his heart. *Relationships, especially with my family, must come first.* He knew what the right thing to do was.

Stopping the tape, Coach jumped up from his seat, slipped on a sweatshirt, and bounded out the front door. "Hey, bud, how 'bout a quick game to twenty?"

Brandon's eyes lit up. "Are you serious, Dad?"

"Of course I am . . . unless you're scared of gettin' beat by your old man?" Coach couldn't resist a little father-son ribbing.

"But don't you still have tape to watch before the game tonight?" Brandon said, bewildered by the sudden shift in his dad's interests.

"Brandon," Coach knelt down and looked deep into his son's eyes. "Listen: You're more important to me than any game will ever be. Never forget that. Okay?"

"Okay, Dad."

"Now, let's see what ya got. My ball first since I'm the oldest." Coach signaled for the ball.

Beaming from ear to ear, Brandon tossed the basketball to his dad and jumped into his best defensive stance. For the first time in his life, Brandon actually felt more important to his dad than the Knights. Crazy as it was, his dad really did seem to be changing.

Chapter 19

Digging Deeper

The guys were riding a high like they'd never experienced before. They had upset three ranked opponents in order to get into the regional finals. And the buzz in Franklin—well, it was back in a big way. Signs were up all over town encouraging the Knights to victory. It seemed the whole town was supporting the Knights as three buses packed with fans made the sixty-minute drive to Madison City, the site of the regional finals. The Knights were just one win away from getting back into the state tournament and were in a place to redeem last year's painful loss in the championship game.

That night on the way to the big game Coach remembered he'd stuck the book Joe had loaned him in his bag. He reached in and pulled it out. *Lead for* God's *sake! Wish I'd learned what that meant twenty years ago,* Coach thought as he opened the book and slowly leafed through the pages. He stopped occasionally to read what insights Joe had underlined in the book and found them to be deeply meaningful nuggets of wisdom like:

> Leadership is a term much too deep and broad to define in a sentence, or even two. Instead, because leadership always involves influence, which in one way or another flows from the character of an individual, we would be much better served were we to begin our own journey

> of leadership by defining just what
> leadership should mean, based on
> the character we believe is best
> to display.

Wow . . . never really thought of leadership like that. Makes sense though, he thought. *How the heck are kids supposed to know what leadership really means with maniacs like me running around, clouding their thinking about what's really important in life and what it should mean to be a leader?* Coach read on:

> Live an aligned life! We should not
> expect to ever lead others to a
> level of true excellence in leader-
> ship, as previously defined, with-
> out being willing to model that same
> level of excellence in our own lives.
> Character influences character.

"Boy . . . learned *that* one the hard way this season," Coach said to himself, continuing to leaf through the chapters.

Finally, near the middle of the book he opened a page and almost fell out of his seat. He looked twice, as he could hardly believe his eyes. There, in the middle of the page, was a perfect illustration of the stick man with the hatchet, heart, and the treasure all included. Coach looked closer at the drawing. *What the—! How*

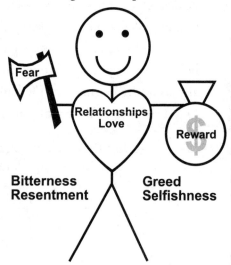

*in the heck did this get here? Grant showed me this . . . at least
the hatchet and the treasure version, almost three months ago . . .
before I ever even personally knew Joe.* If this principle had origi-
nated in this book . . . had Grant read this book? Coach sat
baffled at the sight. He was certain, as he was going through
this process with Joe, this was something completely new. And
yet, it was now apparent that Joe had read about it years ago.
Why didn't he ever say anything? Coach wondered.

He looked up and read the sign: *Madison High School Next
Right.* He knew it was time to get focused on the task at hand.
He closed the book, shoved it back into his bag, and said a
quick prayer as the bus rolled to a stop in front of the doors
to the gym. Who would've ever thought the Franklin Knights
were headed into yet another game where they were the heavy
underdogs, facing the number-five-ranked Marshall County
Mavericks? This would definitely be another huge test for the
Knights.

The game started off rough for Franklin as the Mavericks'
full-court press wreaked havoc on the Knights' back court,
causing them to turn the ball over five times in the first quarter. Fortunately, after settling down and getting a few easy
baskets off their press break, the Knights were able to pull
within six by halftime. As play resumed in the third quarter, both teams continued to pound each other, exchanging
back-to-back dunks and back-to-back threes on two different
occasions.

The energy in the stands was topped only by the energy
and emotion on the court. This game was truly becoming a
Kentucky basketball classic, with only three points separating
the two teams as they headed into the fourth quarter.

The Mavericks continued to beat up the Knights inside

with their powerful front line. And, after two of the Knights' starters fouled out with just over three minutes left, things looked bleak for the fairy-tale ending the guys had been hoping for.

But then, down by four points with the clock ticking away, Billy Conner, desperate to change the momentum, drove the middle of the lane, and, after getting his head nearly taken off by the Mavericks' six-foot-eight center, made an acrobatic swoop, flipping the ball up and over the front of the rim and in. The whistle blew as the referee flew in from the side, motioning frantically.

"Foul! And count the basket!" he yelled, emphatically signaling the call to the scorer's table.

Billy could now pull the team within a point with just under a minute to play. In an instant, the momentum began to shift back to the Knights. After calmly sinking the free throw, the Knights found themselves back on defense, locking down on the Mavericks one last time in hopes of causing a turnover. As expected, up by a point with the ball, the Mavericks went into their spread offense to hold the ball or force the Knights into a foul. And the strategy seemed to work right up until the fifteen-second mark, when Billy got called for a reach-in foul. Coach Rocker signaled for his last timeout.

As the guys jogged to the bench, Coach scribbled on his small marker board. On one half of the board he drew up a three-point play. On the other half, he wrote the word HEART. Then he made his way into the middle of the huddle.

"Guys, if he misses both, we go until seven seconds, then Billy's going to attack and look to score or kick to either of the big guys. If they make just one or both, we run the clock to ten, and Billy gets the ball to Brant on the right wing. Brant, you attack to the right as a decoy looking for a three, then kick back to Billy. Billy—you see this word?" He pointed at the word he'd drawn on the other half of the board. "This team struggled all year faking it. Now it's time to make it! Remember, it's not about me, it's not about you—it's about *us!* Now lead us, my man. We all believe in you. Heart on three. One, two, three!"

"Heart!"

The team broke the huddle and assumed their spots around the charity stripe as the Mavericks' sharpshooter calmly stepped to the line. The first one was up and good. The Knights, now down by two, knew what they had to do: score or go home. Billy thought to himself, *Score or go home. This is my time. This is for my team . . . for us.* As the ball left the shooter's fingertips and floated toward the rim, both teams prepared to surge into the lane. The shot clanked off the back of the rim and off to the right side. Then, settled again on the right side of the rim, it slowly rolled out and into the welcoming hands of a Knight rebounder. Billy jogged up to get the ball, then turned to dribble the ball up the court toward the biggest moment of his basketball life.

The clock ticked down to ten seconds as Billy signaled to set the play in motion. He attacked the left side of the floor then flipped the ball back to Brant, who appeared to be looking for a screen to take the shot going right. Five seconds, four seconds . . . Instead, Brant took one quick dribble right, toward the basket, spun around, and whipped the ball back across the court to a waiting Billy, who immediately upon catching it sent the ball spinning up, up, toward the rim . . . and through the net as the buzzer sounded. The Knights had done it—they had really done it! Against all odds, they were headed for the state finals.

Crazed fans of all ages rushed onto the floor in a frenzy to celebrate the upset that would allow their beloved Knights to play in the final four of the state tournament once again.

After cutting down the nets and receiving the tourney trophy, the team finally made it back to the locker room and settled into their seats on the bench facing their coach.

"Guys, I couldn't be prouder of any group of young men than I am of you all right now, not because you won, but because I know you're out here for the right *reasons*. Reasons that are more about your teammates and those you're impacting than just about you. And it showed. You laid it all on the line tonight, and guess what? Not only do we get to practice another week together, but, guys, if we take care of business, we get to compete for the top spot in the state one more time, together as a team. And that's pretty special. It's special for me, it's special for you, and it's special for our fans. But you know what, guys? There's one fan of ours in particular, one fan who is more responsible for this team's turnaround than most of you will ever know. And even though he had to listen to this game tonight on the radio from a hospital bed, I know . . . I just know he's celebrating right now, even as we speak. I just know he's as excited as anyone could ever be for a bunch of young men. And not just excited that you've won and accomplished a major goal, but excited because he knows what true success is really all about. And now, most importantly to him, he knows that *you* guys understand that, too. So not only are we gonna work our tails off the next couple of days in practice for each other and for our loyal fans, but we're also gonna work our tails off for Joe Taylor, a humble man who has poured his heart and soul into many of our lives." The guys instantly responded with an uproar of support.

"Enjoy this." Coach calmed the guys for just one more moment. "Enjoy this, but remember, we're not done yet. We've got a big challenge ahead next weekend in the tournament, and we need to be focused and ready. Now bring it in here. Heart, on three. One, two, three!"

"Heart!"

As Coach settled into his usual seat on the bus, he glanced at his wristwatch, which read 11:15 p.m. His thoughts again went to Joe. *Ah, shoot. Too late to call him now.* Coach was excited to chat with Joe about the game and about the irony of the illustration he found in the book Joe had loaned him earlier that morning. How strange it was that his friend Grant, of all people, would've introduced him to something like that. Of course, he couldn't wait to talk to Grant now either, but at this hour, everything would have to wait until tomorrow. For now, he would relax a bit and savor the victory on the ride home.

As usual, upon arriving back at the high school, Coach addressed the team briefly regarding the practice schedule he'd planned for Monday and Tuesday of the following week. He also encouraged the guys to get rested up for next week's "experience of a lifetime" and then sent them on their way to enjoy the rest of the weekend.

Chapter 20

Homecoming

In the drive home Coach continued mulling over ideas for the following week's preparations. He wanted to make sure the guys not only experienced the fullness of the thrill of the state tournament, but also enjoyed and fully embraced the process along the way. Most importantly, he wanted them to recognize how this experience aligned with each one of their purposes in life. He was excited to have another week of opportunities to pour into the lives of each of his players, especially his seniors, as this would be their last official week with him as their coach. He was now, more than ever before, determined to maximize his impact on their lives.

Pulling into the driveway just after midnight, Coach shut the car off. He noticed most of the lights in the house were still on, indicating Kathy was still up. Although she was at the game, she and the kids normally didn't stick around too long afterward, especially if there was a long drive home. So usually, by the time he'd made it back to Franklin North with the team and then made the thirty-minute drive home from there, the kids would be in bed and most of the house would be dark. But for some reason, tonight was different.

"Must be waiting up to congratulate me on the win," Coach mumbled quietly to himself as he got out of the car and headed toward the house. He was actually happy to see the lights still on and excited to see Kathy, too, as things at home had improved significantly since his change of heart.

Kathy met him immediately at the front door. In an instant the smile faded from his face. The look on Kathy's face made it clear she was not there to celebrate: something was wrong. He could see in her eyes that she'd been crying, and immediately upon meeting her embrace, he felt the sting of her words fall on his ears. "It's Joe, honey . . . he's gone . . . he's gone. It happened just a few hours ago. They . . . lost him."

"What!" Coach shouted in disbelief. "That can't be right! He said he was fine, that he'd be out in a couple of days." Again Kathy wrapped her arms around her husband. Standing there motionless, he felt his heart drop and tears instantly beginning to burn his eyes.

Even without ever spending any real time with Joe, Kathy had grown to love this great friend of her husband's. Coach had shared numerous stories of their deep and meaningful conversations over the past three months, and she could see how God had clearly put Joe in Coach's life for a reason.

The heart changes in her husband made it obvious: Joe was a very special man and was certainly fulfilling his purpose in her husband's life. But now he was gone—and at what seemed like the most inopportune time possible. They were at the beginning of what should've been one of the greatest weeks of their lives. Instead, now they had to face a great loss in the midst of it all.

Coach's thoughts quickly turned to his players. Had anyone told them yet? he wondered to himself. "I need to call David right away. He . . . he and Brant and the rest of the team will be crushed. Joe was such a rock . . . Why did this have to happen? Why now?" Coach raised his voice in anger and threw his keys across the room. Then, suddenly, the thought of who Joe was came over him. Immediately his anger dissipated. Coach knew this was not how Joe would want him to respond. He also knew he now had to be the rock for his guys.

After gathering his composure, Coach dialed David's cell number.

"Yeah, Coach?" David's cheerful voice came across, accompanied by the sound of fun and laughter in the background.

"Where are you, David?" asked Coach.

"We're at my house. The guys all came over after we got back to the gym. You know . . . we all wanted to hang out tonight to really enjoy this one, as a team."

"You mind if I stop over for a bit?" Coach asked, trying not to tip him off to the news until he could be with them face-to-face.

It was clear David was caught off guard as it was nearly 1:00 in the morning and he was not used to his coach wanting to "hang out" with him or any of his teammates at that hour. "Uh . . . sure, I mean . . . if you really want to—"

"Great. I'll be right over." He closed his phone.

Coach turned to hug his wife again as he felt another flood of emotions flow through his body at the thought of sharing the news with his team. "Joe was such a great man and made such an incredible impact on my life. How could he be gone so fast?" Coach said, tears beginning to stream down his cheeks.

"You need to go be with your guys. They need you, honey," said Kathy.

"I know, I know. I just have to get a grip on myself first," he replied, again trying to contain his emotions.

About fifteen minutes later, Coach walked up to the front door of David's house and rang the doorbell. David greeted him and immediately noticed by the look in his eyes that something wasn't right.

"What's wrong, Coach?" David asked, inviting him in and leading him into the next room where the rest of the team was celebrating.

"I need to talk to all of you," Coach said in a somber tone as they joined the team. In an instant, the room fell silent and all eyes focused on Coach.

"Guys, I . . . I . . ." Coach's voice quivered as he tried to get the words out without breaking down again. "I'm sorry to have to tell you all this, but earlier tonight, in the hospital . . . Joe Taylor passed away. I'm sorry. I'm really, really sorry."

The room was silent as the news sunk in. Brant jumped up. "No!" he shouted. "No! This isn't happening. Not now . . . this can't be happening. Coach, I can't take this!" Brant yelled angrily. "Not with everything else in my life right now. I just can't take this!" Brant dropped to his knees and began to sob. Despite having only met with him for a few months, Brant had grown very close to Joe, given the emotional support and love he had received from him during the time of his personal crisis at home.

David immediately dropped down beside Brant and, wrapping his arms around his teammate, began to cry too. Other guys followed suit. Soon the entire team, including Coach, had gathered in a circle around Brant. For the next fifteen minutes emotions poured out from the kids as they hugged and consoled each other the best they knew how.

The whole scene was surreal. Just a little over four hours ago, the Knights had shared tears of joy with one another in their locker room as they celebrated one of the greatest moments most of them had ever experienced. Now, in a house just a few miles away from their high school, they were sharing one of the most painful moments of their lives.

It just didn't seem possible. Joe was a mentor not only to Brant, but also to a number of other members of the team, including David, whom he had mentored since his freshman year. The boys would meet with Joe weekly in his office to talk and get advice about all kinds of things, from studies, to girls, to college, to home life—anything that mattered to the kids mattered to Joe.

Even the kids who weren't mentored by Joe grew to love him over the years, as he was always striking up conversations in the hallways and always encouraging them to do the right thing. And if someone was hurting, Joe had this magical way of sensing it and always lending a listening ear to help alleviate the pain. But now, that was all over. He was gone. They had lost a great friend and were stunned at the thought.

Around noon the next day Coach woke up in his bed, still in his clothes from the night before. After spending most of the night with the guys, he'd come home around 4:00 a.m. and finally dozed off around 5:00. At first, he'd hoped it was all just a dream, but only minutes after waking, Kathy walked into the room and sat down beside him on the bed. He knew it was real.

"Why does this have to happen?" Coach asked as his wife grabbed his hand and squeezed it.

"I don't know, Steve . . . I just don't know. But I do know this: Joe may be gone, but what he left with you will live on in you forever." Again she gave his hand a loving squeeze.

"I was so lost, so empty . . . constantly searching for the next win to fulfill my life. All at the expense of everything that should've really mattered to me." Coach shook his head as he wrestled with his emotions. "Joe opened my eyes, Kathy. Actually, he opened my heart."

Kathy leaned over and kissed her husband on the forehead and wrapped her arms around him. "I know, honey . . . I know. He opened a lot of eyes, and hearts."

Chapter 21

Walking Through It

As evening approached, Coach sat in his living room trying to study the film from the previous night's game. Despite the nagging sadness looming in his mind, he knew he had to begin to prepare for Friday night's match-up. Deeply engrossed in the process, Coach was startled by the sound of a doorbell. Looking out the side window as he walked toward the front door, Coach tried to catch a glimpse of who was standing outside. It was Grant. He immediately unlocked the deadbolt and opened the door. "Hey, Grant! Come on in," said Coach. "I was just thinking about you a little while ago."

"Really?" said Grant surprised. "Well, I was just thinking about you, too. I wanted to stop by to tell ya how sorry I was when I heard the news about your friend Joe. I know he meant a lot to you, and seemed to really have an impact on your life." Grant, although notably uncomfortable in the moment, tried his best to find the words to console his friend.

"Yeah . . . he really did mean a lot to me, and to a lot of other people, too. I'm gonna miss him and his wisdom terribly," said Coach, gesturing Grant to join him in the living room. "I feel so bad for his family. And when I say family, I mean all the kids at the high school, too. He touched so many hearts . . . so many of my *players'* hearts . . . They were all part of his family. He's really gonna be missed." Coach's head dropped as he began to revisit thoughts of the magnitude of the loss.

"Speaking of hearts, Grant, I have to ask you: where'd you first get the whole 'hatchet-treasure' illustration you shared with me a few months ago?"

"You mean the stick man?" asked Grant with a funny look on his face.

"Yeah, that's the one. Where'd you get it?" asked Coach.

"Hmmm . . . let me think. I know it's been a few years now. Oh yeah, I found the drawing on the whiteboard in our conference room one day. I don't remember why it was up there; I just remember walking into a meeting with a couple of my execs, and there it was, already up on the board. We all joked about it at first, trying to guess what the heck it meant. Then we figured it out, or at least we thought we did— figured it was all about the two things that motivate people." Grant shrugged his shoulders. Then, after thinking about it, he looked at Coach cockeyed, bewildered by the seemingly random question. "Why do you ask?"

"Well, what about the heart. Was the heart there?" asked Coach.

"The heart . . . hmmm . . . I don't remember seeing the heart. All I remember seeing there was the hatchet and the dollar sign. Course to me, those were the only things that mattered." Grant winked at Coach, who knew all too well how Grant felt about the heart.

"Seriously, Coach, why do you ask?" said Grant.

"Joe loaned me a book yesterday that actually had that exact illustration in it. Here all this time I'd kinda credited you with that creative stroke of genius. Except, of course, you left the most important part out—you know, the *heart* of the whole concept. Ya know, Grant, this heart thing—it's had an incredible impact on my guys."

"I'd say! You guys are playing like men possessed. Oh yeah, congratulations, by the way, on last night's big win. If you're saying that whole heart thing has made the difference, then sign me up, 'cause I can always use some more wins in my world, if ya know what I mean," said Grant with a bit of a smirk on his face.

"Yeah, I do know what you mean, and it's not what you think. It's not *about* what you think." Coach paused to gather himself as his thoughts went back to Joe and some of their deeper conversations. "It's so much bigger than just wins and losses . . . so much bigger." The smile faded from Grant's face as he sensed the seriousness in his friend's words.

Coach looked up at Grant before continuing. "I just wish . . . I wish you could've spent some time with him, Grant. There was just something so different about him . . . so deep, so at peace with who he was." Coach's voice faded as he let out a sigh. "Joe Taylor got it—he really got it. He knew why he was here on this earth. He lived his purpose like no one I've ever known."

As the two men sat in silence, Grant shifted in his seat, feeling a bit uneasy about how to respond to his friend. He thought about the words Coach had just said, and for a moment he reflected on his own life, and that question that had haunted him just a few months prior crept back into his head. *Why am I here? Why do I do what I do?* Grant stared at the wooden floor below his feet as if almost in a trance.

After a few moments of uncomfortable silence, Kathy walked into the room holding a couple of cold drinks for the two men. "I thought you gentlemen might like something to drink."

"You must've read my mind, dear. Thanks," said Coach, standing to take the drinks from his wife.

Grant, snapping out of his daze, stood briefly to give Kathy a hug, then sat down on the couch again. "Yeah, thanks, Kathy, and sorry about Joe. I know he meant a lot to you guys."

"Yes, Grant, he did. His life definitely changed ours." said Kathy, glancing at her husband. "I think we should all aspire to have that said about us after we breathe our last breath."

"That's for sure," replied Coach.

Understandably, Monday and Tuesday's practices were two of the most challenging practices of the year as distractions were at an all-time high. The press bombarded the Knights at practice each day and even ran a story about the impact the loss of a team friend like Joe would have on them heading into the state tournament. In addition, David had gotten his cast off and was working diligently on getting cleared to play in the tournament, which sparked even more media buzz. Finally, the funeral for Joe Taylor was to be held in the school gymnasium on Wednesday, forcing the Knights to practice in another gym on Tuesday. But these were still minor distractions compared to the loss of Joe as a friend and mentor to so many on the team, especially Brant, who continued to struggle emotionally over the deep loss. All in all, Coach had his hands full as he, too, dealt with the loss of a great friend while trying to prepare his team for the big tournament ahead.

Because Joe had been such an integral part of so many people's lives within the high school, the administration had decided to dismiss school for two hours during the funeral.

Nearly all faculty, staff, and students were expected to attend the celebration of Joe's life, scheduled for 10:00 a.m. on Wednesday.

At 8:30 a.m. Coach's cell phone buzzed. It was Grant. *Wonder what he wants at this time of the day,* thought Coach as he pushed the green answer key. "Morning, Grant. What's up?"

"Hey, Coach, how are ya?" Grant asked, concerned.

"I'm hangin' in there," replied Coach. "I guess that's what you have to do in times like this. You know what Joe always told me: There's a *reason* for everything."

"Yeah, I do remember talking about that reason thing," replied Grant. "Hey, I'd like to come to the funeral today. You mind saving me a seat?"

"No problem. That'd be great, Grant. Buzz me when you get here, and I'll tell you where I am."

"Perfect. I'll see you then. Thanks." The phone clicked off.

By 9:30 a.m., the gym's 2,800 seats were nearly full. Outside, traffic spilled out onto the street as hundreds of folks from the community made their way in to pay their last respects to the humble janitor. A mountain of beautiful floral arrangements surrounded the stage inside the gym as people walked by the casket one by one for the final viewing of their friend as he lay peacefully at rest. Clad in his neatly pressed janitor's uniform, Joe almost seemed to smile back at the passersby as if to reassure them he was enjoying his reception elsewhere. Behind the stage, a slide show of special moments in Joe's life flashed across a giant screen. Pictures of Joe and his trademark smile with family, students, and friends reminded everyone of the genuine love he shared with so many. To Coach, the entire scene seemed a fitting send-off for such a beautiful person.

Chapter 22

Celebration

By the time Grant buzzed Coach at 9:50 a.m., the gym was packed and the school staff was setting up additional seating anywhere possible to accommodate the line-up of people still filing into the gym. It was obvious to everyone now in attendance that this man had, in some very special way, touched many, many lives.

At around 10:10 a choir filed onto the stage and sang an incredible rendition of "Amazing Grace." Next, Joe's pastor stepped onto the stage and shared two or three short words of encouragement along with a couple of Joe's favorite verses from the Bible. The pastor stated that he wanted to be brief with his words, as there were a number of very special people in Joe's life that had requested to share that day, and he wanted them to have plenty of time. So following one more song by the choir, the first speaker stepped to the stage.

After nervously unfolding two pages of notes, Marcus Williams, the high school's star football player, began his speech.

"Nearly four years ago I was a freshman on the verge of being kicked out of Franklin High. My mom had had about all she could handle trying to raise me, along with my three older brothers. Because I'd kinda gotten lost in the shuffle at home, I got in with the wrong group of kids, and by the time

I was fifteen, I'd begun to experiment with drugs, alcohol, and almost anything else I could find to occupy my time. Although I'd always been a gifted athlete, I had never really developed a work ethic, much less a moral compass to enhance my gifts. By the beginning of October of my freshman year, I'd already been given my last warning; one more issue and I would be out, period. It was do or die time for me. And quite frankly, I didn't really care. I'd already convinced myself I was not cut out for high school and would figure out another way to make it on my own.

"Then one day as I walked out of the school, I felt a gentle hand on my shoulder and turned to see who it was. It was Mr. Taylor, or 'Joe the Janitor,' as some called him. I looked at him cockeyed and thought to myself, 'Now what does this chump want?' And then, with a compassionate look in his eye like I'd never seen before, he spoke these words to me . . ."

Marcus paused as he began to choke up. "I'm sorry," he wiped his eyes and tried to regain his composure. "He looked me in my eyes and said, 'Son, did you know that you were created to be great? I mean really great—something special, something only you can be. Sure hope you don't miss out on that.' Then he began to walk away, but he stopped and turned back to me, 'cause he knew I was stunned by his comment. He turned back to me and said, 'Let me know if I can help you, son, 'cause I'd like to see you be that great person you were really meant to be.' And then he turned back around and headed down the hall.

"At first, I thought, 'Who is this cat? And what does he know about me?'" Again Marcus stopped and fought back the tears now beginning to blur his vision. "But there was something about the look in his eye, something that made me believe everything he said really came from his heart. So, the very next day, thank God, I stopped by his office, and I asked him if he would help me.

"The next thing you know, I'm meeting with this guy once a week at 6:15 a.m. Which was not easy for me, 'cause I'm not really a morning person, as some of you know." A slight grin came across Marcus's face as the crowd chuckled at the comment. "Eventually I learned to look forward to those meetings. For the first time in my life, I was learning what it meant to be a real man. To make a real impact on society. And most importantly, I was learning why I existed, what my purpose was in this life. Mr. Taylor taught me so many great things about myself—self-discipline, work ethic, respect, accountability, responsibility . . . the list goes on. But when he taught me how to find the answer to the question *why* I did what I did, to really find that answer at the core of my heart, it changed everything else about me. I owe all of my athletic and my academic successes over the past four years to Mr. Taylor. So, to Mrs. Taylor I say thank you." Again he choked up as he looked down at Mrs. Taylor sitting in the front row with tears rolling down her cheeks. "Thank you for sharing this great man with us all, because this incredible man was the greatest mentor a boy could ever wish for. I will miss him greatly. Thank you." Marcus, now crying openly, carefully stepped off the stage and walked down to hug Mrs. Taylor while they both shared a moment of remembrance. The gym was silent.

Coach, sitting with his wife and children to one side of him and the team behind him, looked over to his other side where Grant was seated. He noticed tears forming in Grant's eyes. Grant leaned over to whisper to Coach. "Wow . . . what an incredible guy," said Grant, pulling a tissue from his pocket to wipe his eyes.

Next, a tall, slender young man made his way to the stage. It was David Kelton. Pulling a couple of 3 x 5 note cards out of his jacket pocket, he took a deep breath to calm his nerves.

"Good morning. Although to some of you this may not seem like a 'good morning,' I believe it is an appropriate greeting because for as long as I've known Mr. Taylor, to him *every* morning was a good morning. And I am positive that as he looks down on us at this time, as we celebrate a life lived well, once again, it's truly a good morning for him today!

"Like Marcus, Mr. Taylor took me under his wing as a freshman, nearly four years ago." David's voice quivered as the thought of his four years with Joe caused tears to immediately fill his eyes. "And although my path into Mr. Taylor's office was much different from Marcus's, the outcome was much the same.

"Everyone knew Mr. Taylor truly cared about them, that he was a guy who not only did his job as a janitor well, but he did his job on this earth well, too. He knew no strangers. Everyone was a friend from the day they first crossed paths with him. It seemed that Mr. Taylor was always there at just the right time to say just the right thing. He would say things like, 'Hang in there, David, it's all part of the process.' Or, 'Don't give up, David. Remember, there's two pains in this life: the pain of discipline or the pain of regret. So never give up.' Of course, there were many days I hated to hear that one." David shook his head as a half smile formed on his face. The audience chuckled at the comment. "But the thing I appreciated most about Mr. Taylor was that he listened. I remember one day when I asked him how he became so patient, so compassionate.

"He looked me in the eyes and said something like, 'David, so many times in relationships in our hurried society, we fail to listen to hearts. We want to try to fix things quickly so we briefly listen to mouths, and occasionally listen to minds, but very rarely . . . very rarely, David, do we really take the time to listen to hearts. Listen to the hearts of those God has put in your life. That's a big reason you're in the relationship in the first place. Listen to hearts.'"

David stopped for a moment and struggled to start the next line, tears now dropping from his eyes. "Through it all, Mr. Taylor taught me how to truly get the most out of this life . . . how to be the very best I could be. He taught me to build an unshakable foundation for life on a relationship with Jesus, and then to build on that foundation by fostering all the other relationships around me. In other words, he taught me how to live, how to laugh, and most importantly, how to *love*. And although I'll miss him tremendously—I'll miss our meetings, I'll miss seeing him standing in the corner of the gym during our practices . . ." David dropped his head and momentarily broke down at the memory. Tears poured from his eyes as he struggled to contain his emotions. After a brief pause, and after wiping the tears away, he gathered himself long enough to begin again. "Especially, I . . . I will especially miss him this weekend at the state tournament, 'cause I know how much he would've loved to be there. But I also know he'll be smiling down on us as he watches the game from heaven, where, for the rest of eternity, he'll enjoy living, laughing, and loving with the one who taught him how in the first place—his best friend and favorite leader, Jesus. I'll miss you, Mr. Taylor. I'll miss you terribly." David stepped away from the podium and walked back to his seat.

There wasn't a dry eye in the gym, as young and old alike sat in awe of these two young men's testimonies of the impact Joe had made on their lives.

Grant, too, sat in astonishment over the incredible impact a janitor could have on kids. He wrestled with his emotions as his thoughts began to go back to the question *why* again. It seemed so clear to Joe, and to the kids, and especially now to Coach, just how important the answer to that question really was.

Next, a white-haired man appearing to be in his mid sixties and dressed in a perfectly tailored black suit gingerly walked to the podium. For a moment, Grant thought he recognized the man, but immediately dismissed the thought, thinking he must be mistaking him for someone else.

As the man approached the microphone, he opened a black portfolio where it appeared he'd written a lengthy speech to share in honor of the life of Joe Taylor. He cleared his throat as he put on a pair of reading glasses and introduced himself.

"Good morning. My name is Carl Hadington."

Grant's jaw felt like it was going to drop completely off of his face. He shot a glance at Coach to see if he knew who Carl Hadington was. Coach looked back at him with a blank look, obviously unfamiliar with the name.

Carl T. Hadington was the founder and CEO of Servileader, the biggest cleaning company in the country, maybe in the world. He was well known for having built the company on a foundation of unique values and a purpose that separated them from every other company on Wall Street. It was common knowledge that Servileader's people were treated incredibly well, and Carl T. Hadington was the man behind it all. He was a mastermind of industry who combined a unique love for his people with a brilliant shrewdness for the business. And it paid off, as the company he'd led for over twenty years had withstood numerous economic downturns without missing a beat. Because of this, Carl was a highly sought after public speaker and was constantly being interviewed and written about throughout the business community and beyond.

Grant was stunned. *How in the heck did Carl T. Hadington know Joe?* he thought as he sat in amazement. Fortunately for Grant, and many others who were asking the same question, Carl began to explain his background to clarify how he and Joe were associated with one another.

"Please indulge me as I share with you a story of a man both myself and Joe knew very well nearly thirty-five years ago. I was working on the shop floor of my dad's small cleaning tool manufacturing facility in Baltimore, Maryland. We made all sorts of tools for cleaning things—brackets to go on the ends of mops, special mop buckets with built-in strainers. We were small but very innovative, which was what really caught the eye of a young man named Thomas, or as I called him, Tommy. Tommy had started his very own cleaning business and was constantly in our shop looking for a way to gain an edge over the competition. After about two years of building different cleaning tools for Tommy, he and I became friends. For probably another four years, he was in our offices at least two days a week and always seemed to make his way out to the floor to see how I was doing. We were constantly trying some new way to do something, from mopping to window washing—you name it, Tommy would think of it. He had an incredibly creative mind that was always working overtime.

"But then as his business grew, Tommy stopped coming in. We were still doing all kinds of business with him, but for some reason, Tommy never came around anymore. Then one evening, after going about two years without seeing him, I ran into him at a restaurant. He sat alone at the bar, so I invited him to join my family for dinner. He was as cordial as ever, but refused the offer, not wanting to impose upon my family time. At that point I could tell something was wrong. He just didn't look the same. For some reason, a reason I couldn't quite put my finger on, I just sensed something wasn't quite right in Tommy's life.

"Another year or so went by, and although I hadn't talked to Tommy, I often wondered how he was doing. So, one day I decided to visit his office. As soon as I got there, I introduced myself to the gal working the phones at the front desk. She said she would let him know I was there, but warned me not to get my hopes up, as he'd been keeping an extremely busy schedule and would very rarely see anyone without an appointment. I could easily relate to this, growing up working around my father's hectic schedule as he built the manufacturing company he founded. And as of late, I'd been keeping a similar schedule myself. I politely assured her that it was fine, that if he were available, great; if not, no problem. Then I sat down and waited in the lobby. Thirty minutes went by before she finally came back into the room and asked me to come with her.

"As I walked through the halls of the office, I couldn't help but notice all the pictures of Tommy with the who's who of Baltimore. Pictures of Tommy on his yacht fishing with buddies; Tommy at an Orioles baseball game standing beside manager Earl Weaver; you name it, Tommy did it. He was a real mover and shaker, as they say in the business world. My thoughts shifted back to all the great conversations we'd had on the shop floor of my dad's business. I thought about what a vibrant and energetic young man he was when we'd first met. Then, as the receptionist showed me into his office, I almost fell over backward. Tommy had gained a lot of weight, and now, through the haze of a smoke-filled room, I saw my old friend's face . . . and the look, the sad, worn look on his face said a thousand words."

Mr. Hadington paused now. "This was a man who had by the age of thirty-five gained all the treasures the world possibly had to offer. And yet, when I looked into his eyes, I saw an emptiness that at the time I couldn't really understand.

"Well, after exchanging a big bear hug, Tommy and I started reminiscing about old times. But before long, the conversation shifted to our families. His wife had just had their second child, and, unfortunately, had also just kicked Tommy out of the house—for the second, and supposedly last, time. You could tell by the look on his face, Tommy was stressed out and deeply hurt by all that was happening in his life. Even though the business was booming, the money was rolling in, and he'd accomplished all of his dreams, something was missing and just didn't seem quite right.

"After spending over an hour with my long-lost friend that evening, we finally stood up and began to walk out together. When we got to the door, Tommy looked me in the eyes and said something I'll never forget. He said, 'Carl, you've always been a friend that I could trust, and I know you grew up going to church and seem to know God pretty well. Could you do me a favor and ask God to let me know what the heck's goin' on in my life, why everything seems to be so . . . well, so meaningless, even while things on the outside seem so great?

Ask him *why* for me, will ya? And let me know if you get an answer.' Somewhat taken aback by the request, I assured him I would keep him in my prayers and we parted ways.

"Now stay with me, folks, as Joe will be coming into the story soon.

"About two weeks later I got a call from Tommy that literally knocked me off my seat. Immediately upon hearing his voice, I could tell something terrible was wrong. Unbeknownst to me, for months prior, Tommy had been having some health problems he couldn't get figured out. He'd been going through all kinds of tests, but still, nobody seemed to be able to get to the bottom of what was wrong with him . . . until that morning, that is. His doctor had called him at his office and told him he needed to speak to him immediately, face-to-face. So Tommy jumped in his car and made the short drive down to the hospital to see him.

"When he walked into the room, he could tell by the look on his doctor's face the news was not going to be good. And, sure enough, not only did his doctor tell him that he was being diagnosed with a rare disease that attacks the internal organs, but worse yet, to date there was no known cure for the disease, so treatment options were limited. Then his doctor dropped the big one on him. He gave him the news almost every one of us fears: he informed him that he had, at most, six months to live, and realistically, much less than that.

"In an instant, Tommy's world was turned upside down. Nothing in his business or in most other areas of his life and pursuits mattered any more. Over the phone, he described to me how he sat and stared at the floor for what seemed like an hour before he could even get himself to stand up and walk out of the hospital. All alone, he then dragged himself to his car and made the drive home, all the way thinking about the things that really mattered in his life. Then he told me that he walked through the front door, and for the first time in his married life, he noticed the eerie silence of an empty house. He said for the next four hours all he could do was sit in the quiet of his huge lakeside home and ask himself two questions: What had he done with his life that mattered, and why was this happening to him? He knew right then and there, something had to change . . . and fast.

"I sat on the other end of the phone stunned into silence. I couldn't believe what I was hearing. Tommy had always seemed so energetic, so upbeat and healthy, like the world was his candy jar. But now everything seemed to be crashing down on him at once.

"Over the next few weeks Tommy and I got together often, and over that time I saw Tommy's heart go through some incredible transformations. Unlike most of us, Tommy had truly had his eyes opened to what really mattered in life. And although he had to learn this truth in one of the most difficult ways imaginable, it deeply changed who he was determined to be for the rest of his short time here on this earth.

"After he reconciled with his wife, she and the kids moved back in with him and were all trying their very best to enjoy every minute they had left together as a family. Tommy still had responsibilities at work, but his time there was much different than it had ever been in the past. Now he thoroughly enjoyed every minute he was in the office. He was starting to see people differently, starting to see them for who they really were instead of seeing simply what they could do for him. Despite his bleak outlook, Tommy was having the time of his life every day.

"About three months after receiving the news, Tommy called me in for what he said was going to be a serious chat. After explaining all the great things that had been happening in his life, he nearly knocked me off my seat with his request. He wanted me to become a partner with him in his business. Said he needed someone he could trust, and he was certain he could trust me. I was, of course, flattered by the gesture. And, long story short, a couple weeks later, we were partners. But here's the real crazy twist.

"After about three months of working closely together as partners and friends, one day Tommy walked into my office, sat down, and tossed me his keys. He looked me in the eyes and said, 'Carl, I'm finished.' At first, I thought he meant he was going to die—after all, he'd already beaten the doctor's early predictions and was now truly living on borrowed time. But that wasn't what he meant. With tears streaming down his face, he described to me how his life had changed, how although he could never get the lost years away from family and friends back, he had gotten his family back, and now he knew what was really important in his life. He said he couldn't stay in the business because it was too hard for him, in that setting, to develop the relationships with the people around him that he knew he was called to develop. He looked at me and said, 'Carl, you can do this. You've been gifted by God. Your heart's ready. You've been called to full-time ministry right here in this business, five days a week. I feel a different calling in my life right now. But you, never for a minute believe that your call to lead in this business is anything less than a call to full-time ministry straight from God, to use your gifts and talents right here. Use them all for his glory, Carl, for his purpose.'

"Next he informed me that he'd be turning over full control of the business to me and, over time, would basically be giving me sixty percent of the company. He also told me that he was convinced he was going to beat the odds. So, because of that, he would be moving his entire family to another part of the country where they would virtually start over, attempt to live a more normal life. He didn't want his sons to grow up to be like he was, trapped in the pursuit of success, so hungry for it he would sacrifice his own family to get it.

"Of course, Tommy had two strict conditions I had to agree on before signing the papers: First, that I would never tell a soul, as long as he was living, who the real founder of the company was. He had this fear that people might find him out and treat him differently. You know, once they knew he'd founded this great enterprise and had a trust worth millions and millions of dollars. He wanted to quietly disappear from the business scene and have genuine relationships again, not the kind people build as a part of what he called a 'superficial network of friends.' Second, over the past few months, since his heart change, Tommy'd been working diligently on a whole new leadership philosophy that he believed a business should be built upon. All he asked of me was that I work with him privately over the next year or so—assuming he lived that long, of course—to help him perfect that philosophy and then integrate it into the core operating philosophies and principles of the company. I, of course, agreed to both.

"So with that, Tommy entrusted me with the controlling interest of the business he'd built from the ground up, which at the time, around 1980, was worth just over twenty-five million dollars.

"The incredible thing is, eventually, this business would

become the largest industrial cleaning services company on the globe, with annual revenues exceeding nine billion dollars in 2008. Today you know this organization as the Servileader Cleaning Corporation, but in 1980, before the transfer took place, the company still bore the name of its founder, and my friend, Mr. T. J. Taylor. Ladies and gentlemen, I stand before you today to honor the legacy of Mr. Thomas Joseph Taylor, better known to most of you as Joe Taylor, janitor."

The entire gym, with the exception of Mrs. Taylor, Joe's sons, and a few other close associates who knew all along, gasped at the magnitude of the secret Mr. Hadington had just revealed. How could this be? Joe was not only worth millions, he was worth *hundreds* of millions. And yet, he drove a ten-year-old pick-up truck, lived in a small ranch out in the hills of Franklin County, and, what was even more incredible, worked fifty to sixty hours a week, arriving most days around 5:00 a.m. to both prepare for the day and mentor kids.

Grant sat frozen in his chair. The outcome of the story had him literally awestruck. He couldn't believe that this humble man his friend had spoken so highly of had founded one of the most successful businesses in the country. But what really rocked Grant's world was the irony he saw in the parallels between Joe's early life and his own. Was he headed down the same path? Thoughts of his family, friends, and the question *why* all began to roll around in his head again.

For the next ten minutes, Mr. Hadington continued to share about the impact Joe had had on Servileader as a company and on its employees. He also shared about the millions and millions of dollars that had been contributed to homeless shelters, educational institutions, Boys and Girls Clubs of America, and countless other ministries Joe held near and dear to his heart. Joe's contribution to society was much bigger than anyone had ever imagined.

Carl began to bring his speech to a close by sharing the impact Joe had had on him personally. "As friends, early in our careers, we joked and dreamed together. As partners in business, we worked hard together. But as brothers . . ." For the first time that morning, Mr. Hadington struggled to get the words out as tears began to fill his eyes and a lump formed in his throat. "And that's what I truly considered him . . . my brother." He pulled a handkerchief from his pocket and removed his glasses to wipe his eyes in order to see the remainder of his words. "As brothers, we . . . we laughed together, we cried together, we grew together, we prayed together, and finally, we loved life together. Ladies and gentlemen, Tommy Joseph Taylor loved life, not because of what he did for a living, or for what he had gained materially. He loved life because he knew *why* he existed in the first place; he knew his purpose. And he aligned everything he did in life with that purpose, that 'reason,' as he often referred to it. I would be remiss today if I did not, on behalf of my great friend, share with you this great secret to his success.

"My dear friends, Joe figured out what real success was. He had reached the pinnacle of the world's success, and yet, on that peak, he found only loneliness, emptiness, and an insatiable appetite for more. He found the great majority of his friends to be superficial, filled with ulterior motives, and caught in the same pursuits as he was. He found his family to be distracted, disconnected, and headed for destruction. Finally, he found that when his identity was in his wealth, or his title, or his power, or his achievements, all referred to by Joe as his 'treasures,' he could never seem to gain enough to be content, or to find true peace. And so by God's grace he realized, in the midst of that pursuit, he could never be the best he was created to be.

"You see, God blessed Joe. He blessed him by allowing him to face the reality of his short time here on this earth. In fact, Joe would tell you that his greatest blessing wasn't the miracle of a life lived far beyond what the doctors predicted. No; instead, he would tell you that his greatest blessing was the original diagnosis delivered to him over twenty-five years ago that changed the way he saw everything. *That* blessing was what taught him to embrace all the other blessings he'd taken for granted over the course of his life. By living like he was dying, Joe was able to see very quickly that God had put him on this earth for reasons that were far greater than he'd ever imagined, reasons that would live way beyond him—reasons that all started with relationships. That's it, that's at the center of everything God desires for those he created, for each one of us.

"But here's the thing: we have to choose to be a part of this call. Because, you see, God loves us so much that he gives us the choice to love him back, knowing well that it's only through making this choice on our own that we'll ever be able to realize the full benefits of a relationship with him. When he sent his Son to this earth, it was the ultimate sacrifice of love; all he asked of us in return was to open our hearts up to this gift and then allow him to love us and love others through us.

"So, when Joe chose to accept this gift, all of his dreams and pursuits shifted from being self-centered to being others-centered. He now understood his purpose and was determined to align all of his pursuits in life with it. He embraced his position as a janitor and the impact he could have on people through it. He reprioritized his life, placing God at the center of everything he did. Finally, he became passionate about living the life he was created to live, not '*doing*' a certain thing but instead '*being*' who he was supposed to be, who God designed him to be. Joe didn't pursue his passion in life. Joe became passionate about pursuing his purpose in life.

"And that, my friends . . . that is when God took him down a path he'd never in his wildest dreams imagined he'd go, a path filled with peace and joy beyond what he'd ever envisioned possible in life. And a path that others would be inspired to follow way after Joe had taken his last breath . . ." Mr. Hadington stood silently gathering himself before continuing. "Because all of you who were blessed enough to be touched by this great man will, undoubtedly, touch others as a result of his influence on you. And so, the heart, folks, the heart of Joe—his love for his Maker and his love for you and me—will live on forever and ever as long as we choose to be, not just do, but to *be*, as Joe taught us to be.

"As much as I will miss my friend, my brother, Joe Taylor, I cannot selfishly wish him back because I know that, even as we speak, he is walking with Jesus, celebrating all the things that really mattered in his life, that really left a mark: the influence, the relationships, the love that defined the life of this truly incredible man."

Mr. Hadington tried to swallow the lump in his throat as the thought of bidding his friend a final farewell suddenly overwhelmed him. He gazed at the casket where the body of his friend of over thirty years lay resting. "Thank you, Joe, for who you were to us all. You will be missed, my friend. My brother, you will truly be missed." Wiping his eyes, he closed his portfolio and slowly stepped down off the stage.

Glued to his seat, Grant tried to process the depths of this great man's legacy. He was touched deeply by the thought of living a life full of meaning and purpose, purpose far beyond the self-centered achievements he'd been striving for. He tried to imagine what a life with true peace and joy would be like. Of course, he'd had a great life, too. But why was it that he always seemed to want more? No matter what he achieved, it was never really enough.

Tears rolled down his face, not only at the thought of losing this great man, whom he personally never knew, but also from the whirlwind of emotions that seemed to have been trapped inside his heart for years and were just now finding their way to the surface. His heart ached for something of substance, something to fill the void he'd always been able to temporarily fill with some short-term pain killer. And now he knew: Joe's was a life that mattered, that was truly meaningful. He couldn't help but wonder about his own life, and death, and what would be said at his funeral. He shifted uncomfortably in his chair, trying to shake the thought.

As Joe's pastor stepped back to the podium and began the final remarks of the funeral, an unusual hush overtook the crowd as most sat stunned at the revelation of Joe's true identity. It was incomprehensible that a man with so much would sacrifice so much and still gain so much as a high school janitor. Joe was the ultimate example of a servant leader. It was clear that what he had given up paled in comparison to what he had gained.

Chapter 23

The Purpose Effect

After the funeral Coach and Grant walked silently out to the parking lot together. Finally Grant, shaking his head in disbelief, broke the silence. "Wow . . . what a man. What a life."

"Yeah . . . much more to him than any of us ever imagined, huh?" replied Coach. "I mean, I knew there was something special about the guy, but had no idea—I just can't believe it."

"I guess there definitely was more to that whole heart thing you and Joe were so stuck on," said Grant, staring at the ground while obviously reconsidering the concept he'd disputed on numerous occasions over the past three months.

"You know, Grant, when you listen to all those things being said about Joe, you really begin to understand what he meant about the whole *reason for being* thing. I mean, you and I, we can conquer the world, but if at the end of our time . . . at our funerals, if we didn't really make the connections . . . I mean, develop the genuine relationships like we were created to, then in essence, we never really became the best we could be. And that's really what God wants us to be. Why would God, who created the entire universe, make something specifically in his own image and then *not* expect it to be the best it could be?"

Grant, nodding in agreement, added, "And, obviously,

being the best we can be has much less to do with what we do than with who we are."

"Right," said Coach. "I mean, here was a guy who at one time had everything. He had truly arrived in *what* he was doing. And yet, he figured out that he couldn't really be the best he could be without making a change—without putting his love for God and others at the heart of everything he pursued. His influence became not one of comfort and status, but of connection and compassion."

"So let me ask you something, Coach," said Grant, leaning up against his car, his arms folded. "Do you believe that we can ever actually be our best in the roles we've chosen to pursue in our lives. You know, as a coach or a CEO, or any position of status for that matter? I mean, I . . . I guess what I'm really asking is, do I have to throw it all away to really live for God? I mean, most people I know who find 'religion' almost have a mid-life crisis. They go to seminary, then go to work for a church in some capacity, you know, working as a pastor or a missionary. I just don't feel cut out for that kind of work."

Coach tilted his head and sighed as he stood silently for a moment, thinking about his friend's question. Could either of them overcome the pressures of the world's definition of success and live a life centered on relationships instead of achievements? Could they achieve excellence in their chosen profession and still be who God had made them to be?

Coach looked up at Grant. "You know, Grant, only you can answer that in your own heart. The key is—and this is huge—everything has to start with *your* relationship with God, with your acceptance of his gift to you. Right now, he's not interested in all the things you may do in your life. He just wants a relationship with you first. You know, to love you and to have you love him. That's where it has to start. Then, once you do that, all those other things in your life, those other decisions about how to live and what to pursue, they'll all eventually fall into place as the relationship grows. Remember, he tells us that if we genuinely seek him with *all of our hearts,* we'll find him.

"And that's what Joe experienced. He was living a life filled with all the things this world had to offer him. And it was lots of fun, too, for a while, that is . . . until he found out none of the things he pursued really ever satisfied him. He never lived in peace with himself, so he could never really live in peace with others. Nothing was ever good enough. It never satisfied him over the long haul. And you know what? It isn't just the super rich that deal with this problem, Grant. I believe it's everyone's battle, especially in materialistic societies like ours. People can have every comfort imaginable, and yet still be miserable. Surrounded by broken relationships, substance abuse, addictions—you name it, they have it. But when Joe finally found the only thing that really could bring him peace, it transformed him from the inside out, even in the midst of a great crisis in his life. Once he got it, God called him to make a radical change in his life and in his career. And it wasn't into traditional 'full-time ministry,' as so many people in our churches today wrongly define 'full-time ministry.'

"Listen to me, Grant." Coach pointed his index finger in the air in emphasis. "You don't need to be a pastor, a missionary, or a youth leader to be in full-time ministry. All you need is to be committed to living out your purpose in life. You know, glorifying God by loving him and loving others.

"Joe's a great example of this. As we look back on his life and the impact he had and will continue to have for years to come, we can clearly see how God works in and through a life when someone simply pursues their true purpose wherever they are. Joe was a janitor in full-time ministry!"

Coach paused for a few seconds then began again. "Grant, I don't think God's saying to either one of us that we need to quit our jobs and go be pastors or janitors. What I *do* think he's saying is that we need to quit our selfish pursuits and learn to pursue him first. You know, you've heard the verse . . . and I can't even tell you where it's found, the verse that says, 'Seek *first* the Kingdom of Heaven, and all these things shall be added unto you.' Well, in the last few weeks, I've found this to be true. We have to seek him *first*. And seeking him is making the choice to love him, love others, and to allow him to love us, while *we* strive to be the best we can be. Then, with his help, we're better able to love our neighbors and ourselves. This is the key; they come together: love God, love our neighbors as ourselves . . . ourselves, not in a selfserving, proud way, but as broken but forgiven people, created in God's image for his purpose."

Grant stood silent, staring at his feet as he kicked a small pebble back and forth. Tears began to well up in his eyes. "I don't know, Coach . . . I just don't know if I can do all that. It just seems so . . . so . . . well, so against the grain. I'm pretty screwed up, you know. I've lived a life—a life in pursuit of excellence, as the world defines it, of course. And I've *won*. I've won a lot, you know. But now, as I think about my family, my friends—or who I *call* my friends—and my struggles with 'life in the fast lane,' I just don't know if I can do both. You know, lead a company and lead . . . well, lead for *God's* sake."

As the vulnerability started to get to Grant, the tone in his voice changed. He looked up from the ground determined to fight off the emotion of the moment. "I really gotta run, Coach." Opening the door to his shiny black BMW, Grant slid into the plush leather driver's seat. "I just have a lot to process right now, and you . . . you have a state tournament to prepare for, my friend. I shouldn't be bothering you with all my baggage right now."

Coach took a step toward Grant's car and leaned over. "Grant, you're one of my best friends. No game, no matter how big, is more important than you."

Grant shut the door, started the car, and opened the window. "Thanks, Coach, but seriously, I'll be all right. Just focus on bringing that state championship home this weekend. I'll be there cheering for ya. But I really have to run." Still fighting the powerful emotions from the funeral and the conversation with Coach, Grant put the car in gear and drove off.

The Knights' practice later that afternoon was spirited, to say the least. It was clear the entire team had been emotionally impacted by Joe's life and was now even more committed to excellence. What's more, David, with his cast recently removed, was now going through his first full practice since early November. Although he was a bit rusty, it was clear for all to see: the team was thrilled to have him back in the mix.

After practice, Coach briefly talked about some of the key elements of the funeral message and how they related to the opportunity the team had to play in the state tournament. He spoke differently than he had in preparation for past state tournaments. This time he talked more about the opportunities to impact through the experience itself, rather than the importance of winning. He pointed out the significance of each of the guys' life experiences and how this would be just one more opportunity to accomplish something great, as a team, and then make an even greater impact on others as a result. He also talked about how the goal of winning was important, but the purpose of loving each other and being an example of true excellence had to serve as the foundation for that goal to make it worth pursuing in the first place. Win or lose on the scoreboard, Coach made it very clear that they were winners because they now understood not only what they were pursing, but more importantly, how to pursue it and why.

The next two days, as expected, brought a whirlwind of excitement as the media and fans alike were abuzz over the upcoming games. Stories about David's possible return, Brant's roller-coaster season, and Joe Taylor's impact on the team continued to surface in the local newspapers. Now just one team stood between the Knights and a second consecutive trip to the championship game. And despite the distractions, there was no doubt: the guys were ready to get out on the court, lace 'em up, and get after it.

This readiness was confirmed in Friday's semi-finals match-up when right away the Knights jumped all over Lexington Christian by opening up a ten-point lead in just the first quarter of action. Although the gap closed to within five late in the third quarter, the Knights' backcourt was too much for the Crusaders. Behind Brant Stevens's game high twenty-seven points, the Knights cruised to a twelve-point victory, setting up the championship match-up against the heavily favored Louisville Catholic Cavaliers.

Having emerged from a season marked by pain, struggle, and underachievement, the Knights were now playing for the greatest high school basketball prize in Kentucky. Saturday morning newspaper headlines across the state covered the contest as the Knights looked poised to be the Cinderella story of 2008. They'd entered the tournament unranked, and after knocking off four ranked teams along the way, they would now face the ultimate test: number-one-ranked Louisville Catholic.

The bus ride to Lexington's Rupp Arena was fairly quiet as most of the guys sat with headphones in their ears, doing what each would typically do to get mentally prepared for a big game. The serious looks on their faces told the story: they were focused and ready for the task at hand.

After sitting in the silence of his own thoughts for the first few minutes of the trip, Coach opened his briefcase and grabbed the book Joe had loaned him less than a week ago. He began to leaf through the tattered pages looking for one last bit of inspiration before heading into the game. He couldn't help thinking about his friend as he studied the many underlines and notes Joe had added to the pages. Again, a few underlined sections jumped out at him as he glanced through the pages. Sections like the one on responsibility:

> Leadership is one part influence and two parts responsibility: As people of influence, we must always take responsibility for our contribution to problems that arise around us.

Joe had definitely helped him see the importance of this one in the situation with David. He knew it would change the way he viewed his responsibility as a coach forever.

As he continued to read small sections, he found his way to the final page of the book. Here the author summarized the book's central theme with a challenge to the reader:

In accepting our primary purpose for existence, to love God with all our heart, mind, soul, and strength and to love others as ourselves, we come to the realization that our leadership, or our influence, is a vital component of fulfilling our purpose here on this earth. <u>This influence on others, when genuinely motivated by love, is essentially how God works through us.</u> When we have truly grasped this truth about our purpose, we'll take on a sense of urgency in helping others find this truth, too. <u>We are called to leadership because we are called to influence others in the right ways and for the right reasons. Genuinely loving those God has placed in our life's path is the starting point of that influence.</u> Add to that a commitment to <u>using every ability God has given us to be the best that we can be, regardless of what we do or where we are, and you have a recipe for leadership success!</u> That is really what leading from the heart is all about. Living and leading from the heart, as God designed it, means our relationships are always central to our actually being the best that we can be. <u>We can accomplish everything possible in this world, win every game we compete in, build the greatest business, or graduate with every degree imaginable, but if at the end of the day, when the</u>

> chips are called in, we failed in
> the relationships God designed us
> for along the way, we never really
> became the best we could've been,
> plain and simple.

As he finished the last sentence, he sighed. *Wow . . . that make's a lot of sense. If I truly love God and others in this way, I'll want to share this truth, because I know it's the only way any of us can really ever be our best. And the best way to share this message is to actually* be *this message—be* a person who loves others and a person who strives to be the best that they can be while loving others, too. That's what real excellence in leadership is all about . . . Coach thought these things as he glanced out the window at Rupp Arena, just ahead on the left. *And that's exactly what these guys need to hear before this game. Being our best—maximizing our influence on others—can only happen when we put our relationships at the center of whatever it is we're striving for.*

Coach closed the book, slid it into his suit pocket, and pulled out his notepad to jot notes to himself in preparation for what he now believed would be the most important pregame speech of his life.

Chapter 24

The Final Test

A s the clock on the scoreboard showed six minutes, the players headed into the locker room for their final pre-game instructions. The Knights' assistant coaches went over key match-ups and quickly reviewed a few important sets designed to exploit the Cavaliers' defense. Now it was time for Coach to give his final pregame speech of the year. Win or lose, this was it, and Coach knew in his heart this would be different—vastly different from any speech he'd ever given before.

"Gentlemen, I want you to take just a second and look around you at your teammates. Look at each one of them. I want you to think about all the practices you've gone through together. Times of great fun and great pain . . . times you've pushed each other, encouraged each other, and even yelled at each other—all together." Coach scanned the room intensely as the players glanced at one another, obviously struck by the memories. "I want you to think about all the bus rides *together,* the dinners you've shared at each other's homes *together,* the classes you've had *together,* all the great memories you've shared *together.*" He paused again to give them a few more moments to reflect.

"Next, I want you to think about all the tears you've shed *together.* Tears when your senior leader got the news he was done for the season, or tears when a teammate decided to hang up his shoes because his home life was falling apart. Or tears when a season filled with high expectations appeared to be falling apart faster than you imagined it could, and your dreams falling with it. And finally . . ." Coach paused for a second to fight the lump forming in his throat. "Finally . . . I want you to think about the tears you shared when you heard the news about Mr. Taylor . . . a friend who touched each of our lives in a deep way. I want you to think of the tears you shed at his funeral, as you saw your teammate share his heart and his pain in front of more than three thousand people. And you all sat sharing in that pain . . . *together.*

"Gentlemen, that is what sports is really all about. Sharing life's victories and life's defeats *together.* And learning how to be *together,* to function as a team *together.* And you know what? That is what *life* is all about, too. We've talked a lot this year about striving to be the best we can be. About hard work and commitment, about respect and responsibility, about account-ability, perseverance, and self-discipline—all great things we can learn from sports that we could and should use for the rest of our lives. But none of that will matter if you don't build your life on the foundation of your purpose—as Joe used to say, 'your reason for being.' And guys, by now, I know you all know this, but your reason for being isn't to play basketball. And it's not to be a great student, a great lawyer or doctor or whatever you may have dreams about being, for that matter. Men, your primary purpose in this life is to love. Love God, your family, your friends, your teammates, and yourself while you strive to be your *best!* That's where everything must start. I know it sounds crazy for me to be reminding you guys of this before we play for a state championship, but you know what?

If you don't understand this before you leave this locker room tonight for the last time, I've not done my job as your coach.

"At the beginning of this season, I didn't genuinely love as I was designed to because I'd never really learned the truth of what love or leading from the heart was all about. But now, thank God and our dear friend Joe, I know. And that . . . that's all I care about tonight. The reason I told you to look around you is to help you remember what's really important, and that's the relationships you have with your teammates and the example you display to others as a result of those relationships."

Coach's voice began to get louder as his emotions swelled. "Lord knows we've been through a lot this year, especially when all I was really focused on was winning. But tonight . . . *tonight,* guys, I want you to forget about winning this game! I want you to forget about individual points, or rebounds, or whatever distractions the competition lures us into making our priority!" Every eye in the locker room was fixed on Coach as his voice raised another notch. "Tonight, gentlemen, I want you to play from the heart. I mean, *really* play from the heart! Just like Joe taught us. The only thing that matters is the relationships we leave behind us. Guys, if you really love each other, I mean *really* love and care about your teammates, you'll lay everything you got on the line tonight! You'll leave every ounce of everything you have deep inside your heart on that floor! And in the end, regardless of what the scoreboard reads, we will walk off the floor as *winners! Winners!* Now let's get it done tonight, guys! One last time—together! Heart on three. One, two, three!"

"Heart!"

In a burst of emotion, the guys broke the huddle and stormed out onto the court to the band's rendition of the school fight song. There was no doubt: win or lose, the Knights had already won because now they knew why they were playing. They understood fully the purpose behind everything they were pursuing, and it was a purpose much greater than all the wins in the world. Now the will to win was back, the love for their teammates was back, and the passion—it was back in a bigger way than ever before.

From the tip-off at center court to the final buzzer, the game lived up to all the hype and more as the two powerhouses traded leads countless times over the first three quarters of play. All 18,000 frenzied fans were on their feet as the Knights and the Cavaliers headed into the final two minutes of regulation with the score tied. Although Coach had put David into the game briefly in the first half to give his starting center a quick breather, he hadn't been off the bench since, due to his obvious rustiness. But with 1:48 left to go in the game, Clark Gavin, David's 6' 5" sophomore replacement, fouled out, leaving Coach with no choice but to go with his senior center.

Just prior to the one-minute mark, Billy Conner came off a screen set at the elbow to knock in a shot, giving the Knights a two-point lead. Immediately, the Cavaliers answered with a quick lay-up after Blake Grissom, their All-State point guard, took the in-bound pass coast to coast and swooped over David's outstretched arms for an amazing finish under the hoop. With just over forty seconds left to play, Coach Rocker decided to run the clock down for the last shot. After getting the signal to hold the ball for the last shot from his coach, Billy cautiously dribbled up the floor, then passed the ball to Brant, who was waiting in the opposite corner near the half-court line. Opting out of a timeout, Coach called out a play to Billy from the sideline. With twelve seconds left, Billy signaled for the start of the set. Brant, coming off a screen on the baseline, was supposed to catch the ball and then curl off a ball screen set at the elbow, where he could either shoot or pass to David on the way to the basket.

Everything seemed to go perfectly, just as it was designed. Brant came off the screen and faced a wide-open basket with just eight ticks left on the clock. He squared to the basket, jumped into the air, and sent the ball spinning off the ends of his fingertips toward the basket. Suddenly, out of nowhere, a towering Cavalier swatted the ball from its course and into the hands of a waiting teammate, who immediately called timeout with five seconds left on the clock.

In utter disbelief, Brant hung his head as he jogged over to the Knights' huddle, feeling the burden of a possible loss weighing heavy on his shoulders. He'd let his teammates down. Before Coach could say a word, David spoke up.

"Brant . . . look at me. That was my fault. I had the screen and released him too soon. Don't for a second think that was your fault. And don't for a second think we're done! They *will not score,* guys, hear me? This game is about more than just winning. We all have to have each other's backs. This is about everything we've gone through *together.* Like Coach says, this is not about me or you—this is about us together. One heart. They *will not score!*"

Coach stepped to the center of the circle. "I'm proud of you, men. You know why you do what you do, so it's really simple from here on out. Match-up and get a stop. Dig deep within your hearts—and get a stop! On three, heart. One, two, three!"

"Heart!"

The Cavaliers lined up for what looked to be a quick pass

to Grissom to set him up to do his thing. And sure enough, that's exactly what they did. Once the ball was in Grissom's hands, he turned and raced for the basket. Everything seemed to move in slow motion as Grissom weaved his way past the outstretched hands of multiple Knights defenders, all trying to help Brant as he attempted to stay with the elusive point guard. The seconds ticked away: four . . . three . . . Around the top of the key, Grissom faked to his right, sending Brant off-balance to his left, giving the flashy guard just enough space to spin back around toward the basket for a wide-open lane—until David, anticipating Grissom's spin back to the middle, stepped into the lane with outstretched arms and planted both feet firmly on the ground in support of his 6' 9" frame. There was nowhere for Grissom to go but right into the gut of the towering center, clearly set and waiting for him as the clock wound down. Two . . . one . . . The collision was bone crushing, sending David flying backward and both men to the floor as the ball sailed up high off the glass.

The buzzer sounded almost simultaneously as the whistle blew. And then . . . the ball bounced off the front of the rim, the back, and settled into the bottom of the net. As the referee ran in toward the center of the play, Cavaliers fans instantly began their celebration as the scoreboard flashed a two-point lead for their team with no time left on the clock. But then, after a brief gathering to confirm the ruling, the crowd fell silent as the referee signaled in the call.

"Player control foul, number four, after the shot left his hands. Count the basket. Number thirty-two, shoot two." The referee signaled for both coaches to meet at center court.

They both knew, even though it was at a critical juncture of the game, the official had made the right call. David's feet were clearly set and his position established well before Grissom bowled him over. However, Grissom had released the ball before making contact so the basket would count. The Cavaliers did indeed have a two-point lead, but now David, the senior who'd not shot a free throw in a game situation for over two months, would have two shots to determine either a loss or a tie that would keep the Knights' state championship hopes alive.

After briefly explaining the call to the coaches, the teams walked off the floor to their respective sidelines as David slowly walked toward the free-throw line at the other end of the floor. His mind was flooded with the magnitude of all that rested on his shoulders. And then, in a surreal moment of quietness in the midst of the uproar of the opposing fans, the crowd noise all seemed to fade away. Almost immediately, his thoughts went to his purpose, why he was there at all.

As the ref handed him the ball, he said quietly, "Good luck, kid."

David shot back confidently, "No such thing as luck, sir. There's a reason for everything." Stepping to the charity stripe, David gave the ball three quick dribbles and let it fly. After hitting the front of the rim and bouncing off the backboard, the shot settled through the bottom of the net.

As the ref stepped in to grab the ball, David stepped backward and glanced over to the stands. To his amazement, he caught the eye of Mrs. Taylor, standing with her hands clasped in front of her, tears rolling down her face. He knew what she was thinking, how proud Joe would've been if he could see this. And he also knew at that moment, as he felt a warm breeze come over his shoulder, that Joe was watching, too. He could feel it. He looked straight into the eyes of Mrs. Taylor and gave a quick wink and nod, as if to tell her that this one was for Joe, for all he had meant to him and their team. This one was for him.

David took a deep breath in attempt to calm himself as the referee handed him the ball to shoot the free throw that would determine the Knights' championship destiny. As David's heart pounded, he took his normal three dribbles, then sent the ball sailing up, off his fingertips, and into flight toward the basket. A hush fell over the crowd. Time seemed to stand still as David's final free throw floated up, through the air toward the hoop.

Chapter 25

What Really Matters

As the players made their way to the bus long after the final buzzer sounded, Coach sat alone in the locker room, quietly reflecting on the most incredible season he'd ever experienced. The locker room was cleaned up, and most of the fans had made their way out of the building. Only he was left now, alone in the silence of his own thoughts.

He stood up to walk out of the locker room when the door gently opened and Mrs. Taylor walked in. Her eyes, though noticeably swollen and tired from the incredible range of emotions she'd gone through over the last ten days, were still filled with a peace and calmness that seemed to transcend all understanding.

Without saying a word, she walked over to Coach and wrapped her arms around him with a motherly embrace as they both began to cry, reminded of the thought of Joe's missing this final game. After a few minutes, Mrs. Taylor, placing her hand gently on Coach's cheek, looked into his eyes and said in her normal quiet, encouraging way, "Joe would be so proud of you, young man . . . so proud of you."

"I know. I just wish he were here right now." The two of them sat quietly for a few more moments trying to collect themselves before Coach spoke up. "Listen, before I forget again, I've been wanting to give this back to you." He reached

over and picked up his suit jacket lying across the bench beside
him. From the inside pocket, he pulled out the old, worn copy
of the book Joe had loaned him. "I haven't read the whole
thing yet, but based on all the things I have read, I think Joe
taught me everything that's in this book. I kept it with me
tonight in the game for good luck, you know?" Coach handed
the book to Mrs. Taylor.

She held the tattered old book in front of her with both
hands and gazed affectionately at the cover as if gazing into
the eyes of a dear, old friend. Then she pulled the book close
to her chest and looked back at Coach. "Honey, this book is
very special to me. It's been around our house now for nearly
twenty-five years. I've put it away literally hundreds of times,
only to find it out, lying on the armrest of Joe's easy chair,
or on the nightstand, or in any number of spots around the
house. He was always reviewing it and marking it up."

She lowered the book now so they could both see the cover.
"You know this book really is a glimpse of my Joe's heart?" she
said, holding the book out with her weathered hands. "Young
man, you were very special to Joe . . . even before you knew
him. He spent many hours praying for you. He always knew
you'd come around. Coach . . . I want you to have his favorite
copy of this book. As you can see, it spent a lot of time with
him over the years and really meant a lot to him. But I want
you to have it."

Coach looked up at Mrs. Taylor, whose gaze was still fixed
lovingly on the book. "Uh, Mrs. Taylor, I . . . I don't know
what to say. I mean, I'm honored . . . but are you sure?"

She looked up from the book and into Coach's eyes once
again. "Oh, honey, yes. I'm sure. I'm just sure he would want
you to have it. It was special to him, but you know what? Not

nearly as special as the relationship he had with you, and with all the boys on that basketball team. He would want you to have it to make sure that when times get tough, you always remember the *reason* for what you do. And you teach those boys to do the same thing. And don't you worry about me. I have other copies of the book at home, anyway, so I won't forget what's inside." She smiled and winked at Coach as she handed him the book, stood up to give him one more hug, then slowly made her way out the door.

Coach looked down at what he considered to be a priceless treasure that was now his to keep. Not only were the contents of this book valuable to him, but the fact that this was his dear friend's copy—a gift, not only *from* the heart, but truly *of* the heart—made this book special beyond description.

He stared down at the worn-out cover, running his fingers across the title of the book as the memory of Joe standing in the corner of the gym with his trademark smile warmed his heart. And then, to his surprise, the small print across the bottom of the cover grabbed his attention. The words that he noticed now for the first time sent a shiver up his spine. He looked closer to be sure he was reading right. Sure enough, he wasn't seeing things. There, written across the bottom of the book, barely legible from the wear and tear, was the name of the author: *T. J. Taylor.*

Coach couldn't believe his eyes. No wonder this book seemed so much a part of everything Joe believed deep within his heart. No wonder he felt such a strong connection with the words written inside. These actually *were* Joe's words, Joe's thoughts. *No,* Coach thought, *this was actually Joe's heart . . .* This book was a picture of the very heart of his dear friend.

Coach immediately began connecting the dots. *This must*

have been the "leadership philosophy" Mr. Hadington was talking about that Joe wanted him to utilize as the core of Servileader's business. No wonder the hatchet-heart-treasure concept mysteriously showed up on Grant's conference room whiteboard. One of Servileader's cleaning staff must have purposely planted it there, staying true, of course, to the principle of sharing the truth of the heart. Thoughts raced through his mind as he stood up to leave the locker room and join the rest of the team for the bus ride home.

As he walked across the gym floor to the waiting bus, he heard a couple of familiar voices calling out to him from the bleachers. It was Brandon and Kylee, waiting patiently for him with their mom.

"Hey, Dad! Wait up! Mom let Grandpa drive the car home so we could ride with you guys on the bus back to Franklin tonight . . . okay?"

"Absolutely!" Coach said, as he scooped Kylee up into his arms, kissed his wife, and headed out through the tunnel toward the exit. As they boarded the bus together, the team immediately got quiet, anticipating a few words from their coach before the long ride home.

"Guys, this was indeed a very, very special night. I am so proud of you. You displayed an incredible will to be your best, an incredible passion for the game, and finally, you showed incredible love for your teammates. You truly played your hearts out tonight, in every way imaginable. But more importantly, gentlemen, more importantly than any game we played this year, or win or loss we experienced, or any practice we pushed through—more importantly, gentlemen, tonight you not only *played* from the heart, you *led* from the heart. You truly led from the heart!

"As we've talked about all year, leadership is a critical component to the success of any team. But because leadership is such a broad subject, it means a lot of different things to a lot of different people. Some of those things are good . . . and some of those things are not so good. So, before you set out to lead in anything, you have to define what leadership means to you, based on your own core beliefs. And although I won't go into all the different things that I believe should be a part of your definition, tonight, before we part ways, I want to remind you one last time of what Joe taught us about leadership and about building the *foundation* for it in our own lives.

"Remember the *reason* Joe always talked about? You know, understanding *why* you were created and then aligning everything you do with that reason for being? That's where leading from the heart starts! And it's all about relationships—every relationship around you.

"Tonight you chose to live that out. You didn't come here just to win a state championship, or look good to the fans, or even to bring glory back to that Knights jersey you took off a few hours ago, some of you for the last time. No . . ." Coach shook his head as he looked into the eyes of his players. "No. You came here tonight for a much *bigger* reason. Tonight, guys, you came here driven, together, by a purpose. Not a purpose that was self-centered, or narrowly focused, or designed to build your basketball career or your ego. No. This was a purpose that would last way beyond the sound of the final buzzer and way beyond your time as a basketball player. Gentlemen, you played tonight for the purpose of love. Love of the game, love of the things within the game, but more importantly, love of the things that really matter in life. Like the love you've all developed for each other as you've gone through this season. And the love you all had for Mr. Taylor, as a mentor and a friend. Even the love you have for those you know you're influencing through your actions on and off the court, like these little ones seated next to me." Coach glanced down at Brandon and Kylee as Kylee looked up at him with a shy grin on her face.

"Guys, leadership is all about your influence. And when you, as leaders, truly decide to lead from the heart with a genuine desire to fulfill your purpose, you immediately jump on the path to being the type of influence you were *called* to be. Tonight, I saw you do just that. I saw the right attitude in the face of great adversity. I saw guys encourage one another when times got tough. I saw guys diving on the floor, sacrificing blood, sweat, and tears to lay everything on the line for the love of their teammates. I saw guys take responsibility for mistakes, even when they weren't completely at fault. I even saw guys go to the floor battling over a loose ball and then extend a respectful hand to their opponent to help them up after the play. Tonight, I saw leadership from the heart from an incredible group of young men.

"The greatest leaders in history understood this type of leadership. They understood the responsibility that comes with influence. They not only knew *what* they were leading, or *how* they should lead, but they knew *why* they led. They led for a purpose, a purpose more about others than about themselves. Men, if you hear nothing else from me tonight, at least hear this: Live your life committed to your purpose, a purpose more about others than about yourself.

"Finally, men, I want you to know that I love each and every one of you dearly . . ." The thought of speaking to this group of kids for the last time suddenly hit Coach. Fighting a lump in his throat, he continued. "This season has changed my life forever, and each of you played a special role in that process . . . and I thank you all for that. My hope for you now, as you go through life, is that you'll always remember to lead as Joe taught us to lead, in the right way and for the right *reason*. Know *why* you lead, gentlemen. Lead from the heart. Lead . . . for *God's* sake!"

Afterword

Joe's Book

I realize it's not the norm to close a book with an intro-
duction to another book. However, to completely exclude
Joe's book from this text would be to exclude one of Joe's
most important last wishes, which was to share the heart of
his leadership philosophies with his family and friends.

Although the heart of Joe's philosophy begins with building the foundation of leadership on one's purpose, it certainly
doesn't end there. You see, Joe believed that the best leaders
worked intentionally to build an entire structure for leadership
that flowed from that foundation of purpose. Eventually, that
structure would serve as the framework from which all activi-
ties within the team (or organization) would operate. *Finding
the heart* set the foundation, but *defining, aligning,* and *refin-
ing* the heart of the team provided the structure for leadership
excellence along the way. Leaders within this structure not only
understood *why* they pursued what they pursued, but also *what*
they were to pursue and *how* they were supposed to pursue it.

Joe's greatest passion was to help the individual, the family, the team, and the organization become the best they could
be by guiding them to a place deep within their own hearts to
discover who they were really meant to be and then escorting
them on to a place of true success. Hopefully, his book will
inspire you to join him on that journey.

Lead
for
GOD'S
Sake!

T.J. Taylor

A Note from Joe

Why do you do what you do? Do you ever ask yourself that question? Truth is, most of us, at some time or another during our lives, do. What's more, we typically take that question one step further by also asking ourselves why we even exist. Or, put another way, what's my purpose? It seems we all have that question planted somewhere deep within our hearts. The crazy thing is, most of us go through life without ever really finding the answer. Which wouldn't be such a tragedy, were it not for the fact that without an understanding of and commitment to one's true purpose, one can never really be the best they were meant to be! And if we're not being the best we can be, we won't be leading others to be the best they can be either.

Make no mistake: there are numerous ways to be effective in your leadership, many of which I plan to share with you in this book. But if your leadership isn't built on the foundation of your purpose first, your reason for existence, you will never become the best you were meant to be. And the same holds true for your team. If they're not clear on why they exist and pursue what they pursue, they'll fall short of ever being the best they were meant to be, too.

So it's with this thought in mind that I write this book, to, first, help you recognize your primary purpose, your true reason for existence, by FINDING your heart. Then, upon doing this, I want to help you build every other part of your leadership and life upon that foundation by helping you DEFINE,

ALIGN, and REFINE the heart of your leadership. Plain and simple, I want to challenge you to take all aspects of your leadership to a new level, leading from the heart, not only with a passion for your pursuits, but with a passion for those you have the opportunity to lead in your pursuits. For it is in the midst of those pursuits that you will discover the true essence of success in this life and in so doing become the best that you were meant to be.

You see, there was a point in my own life where in the eyes of the world, it seemed I was the best I could be. I had truly arrived. I had all the money I ever dreamed of having. I'd built my dream home, and my business had grown beyond my wildest imagination. I'd truly gained every treasure the world had to offer, and yet I was lonely and miserable inside. I had many acquaintances, but no true friends. I guess you could say I had everything, but really had nothing. Fortunately for me, on a cold winter day just a few months before writing this, I was given a second chance, not because I won the lottery or broke into stardom, or found the fountain of youth. No, on that day my doctor told me that I had less than six months to live. And although I struggled for the first few weeks, over time I began to realize that I had not been told when I was going to DIE; rather, for the first time in my life, I'd been shown how I was to LIVE.

Everything changed after I received this news. For the first time, I began to see life how I was supposed to see it: as a gift. A gift that was given to me to do anything

I wanted with, but a gift that would only ever be fully utilized when shared with others and lived out for the purpose for which it was given. Life is indeed an incredible gift from God. Nonetheless, it is a gift he can snatch away in a heartbeat. It is a gift, undeserved, not a reward. And I found that God's gift of life was best understood as it related to his gift of eternal life, made possible through the death and resurrection of his Son, Jesus. And so, upon accepting his gift of eternal life, I made the choice to use whatever was left of my life on this earth for his purpose, and that is when I found true success.

I am convinced that if you choose this same pursuit, you too will eventually find success. Not necessarily success in the eyes of the world, but success in the eyes of those who matter most in life: The eyes of a daughter, who looks up at you in anxious anticipation when asking you to read to her. Or the eyes of a son, who excitedly begs you to play catch with him in the backyard. Or even the eyes of a wife, who sometimes just needs you to sit and listen to her share her heart. Or, finally, in the eyes of any other folks God has put in your path of influence, the ones you listen to when they're hurting, encourage when they're down, and help when they're in need. Those are the eyes of the ones who really determine your success in this life. Because you never know when your last interaction with any of them just might be your LAST interaction with any of them.

My friends, more than likely by the time you read this little book, I will have gone home to be with the One who so graciously created me. And although I will not be with you in body, I will always be with you in heart. I know this because whether I live for six months or for sixty years, I will live and lead the rest of my life committed to loving others in alignment with my purpose above all else. My hope is that this book will not only inspire you to join me in this incredibly rewarding journey, but that it will also help you inspire others to join us in this journey, too. A journey committed to living and leading for the ultimate purpose—for God's sake!

Acknowledgments

I firmly believe that the greatest things in life come about as a result of two or more people in relationship working toward the same goal. From world championships to stellar sales presentations to healthy happy families . . . team achievements are the best. And, although most would probably consider writing a book an individual achievement, I most certainly don't!

There were many, many folks whose encouragement along the way contributed to the completion of this book, and for that I am grateful. However, I must say that there were a specific few who truly took it upon themselves to selflessly go deeper and to be a part of the team that made sure this book was created as it was supposed to be.

With this in mind, I must first and foremost thank my wife Traci, who, although she had to put up with listening to the "story behind the story" literally hundreds of times, encouraged, supported, and loved me as only a wife could over the course of the entire project. Next, I have to thank my children, Kaden and Kira, for the many times they came into my office and sat on my lap to see how things were going, to give me a hug and kiss, or even to test the sincerity of the words I was writing by checking my priorities.

Next, I have to thank a group of great friends who bravely read through the earliest versions of the story and offered me valuable wisdom, insights, and encouragement. These men were the heart of a great team that helped make this story what it is today. John Forbes, Dick Armington, John Weldy, and Jonathan Schindler—you guys all played a huge role in this process and are truly loved and appreciated!

In addition, I must thank Rob Henschen, John and Traca Beck, Mike Trainor, Angie Stillson, Christi Zurcher, and my incredible grandmother, who also read early versions of the manuscript and encouraged me to forge ahead.

I am also grateful to my brothers—Trent, Troy, Tad, Ryan, and Todd—who either offered their creative insights or heart-felt encouragements throughout the process. It is truly awe-some to know that you are believed in by such a great group of men!

Next, I need to thank a very special group of individuals who over the course of my life have impacted me in powerful ways through their friendship, encouragement, mentorship, and example. Relationships powerfully influence who we are at the very core of our being. Thus, the principles conveyed in this book in many ways can be traced back to these incredible friends and their positive impact on my life. Mike Lightfoot, Todd Cleveland, Dick Armington, Jeff Zurcher, Scott LaPlace, David Rivers, Mark Lantz, Ford Taylor, Dave Engbrecht, Tom Arington, Monty Williams, John Forbes, Doyle Stump, Paul Hassler, and Jimmy Ritchey. Of course, I feel very blessed to also be able to thank the most significantly positive influences in my life, my mother and father.

Finally, I am honored to thank the true inspiration of this book, my Savior and loving friend, Jesus Christ. This story was a gift from Him . . . I'm just the guy He allowed to wrap it up and deliver it.

Were you impacted by the message in
LEAD . . . for God's Sake!?

Then connect with us today at
www.leadforgodsake.com to:

- learn more about living from the foundation of your purpose

- sign up to receive leadership insights and encouragements from the author

- learn more about workshops, seminars, or other leadership programs designed to help your business, team, or organization

- find out how you can receive bulk discounts on book orders for your business, group, or organization